Larry,

God bless you, always—

Louis Tee

Larry,
Do ethics, drink beer!

DOING

in a SHRINKING WORLD

RIGHT

DOING
in a SHRINKING WORLD
RIGHT

How Corporate America Can
BALANCE ETHICS & PROFIT
in a Changing Economy

LOUIS DeTHOMASIS *and* **NEAL ST. ANTHONY**

GREENLEAF BOOK GROUP PRESS
www.gbgpress.com

Published by Greenleaf Book Group Press
4425 S. Mo Pac Expwy., Suite 600, Longhorn Building, 3rd Floor,
Austin, Texas, 78735

Distributed by Greenleaf Book Group LP

For ordering information or special discounts for bulk purchases, please contact
Greenleaf Book Group LP at 4425 S. Mo Pac Expwy., Suite 600, Longhorn Building,
3rd Floor, Austin, TX 78735, (512) 891-6100.

Design and composition by Greenleaf Book Group LP
Cover design by Greenleaf Book Group LP

Publisher's Cataloging-In-Publication Data
DeThomasis, Louis.
   Doing right in a shrinking world : how corporate America can balance ethics & profit in a
changing economy / L. DeThomasis and N. St. Anthony. -- 1st ed.
     p. ; cm.
   Includes bibliographical references and index.

   ISBN-13: 978-1-929774-39-5
   ISBN-10: 1-929774-39-7
1. Business ethics. 2. Social responsibility of business. 3. Corporations—Moral and ethical aspects.
4. Corporate profits—Moral and ethical aspects. I. St. Anthony, Neal. II. Title.
HF5387 .D393 2006
174/.4
2006926028

Printed in the United States of America on acid-free paper

06 07 08 09 10 11 12   10 9 8 7 6 5 4 3 2 1

First Edition

To Bill and Jean Hendrickson
for their unwavering support and commitment
to ethical leadership, education, and values;

and

Saint John Baptist de la Salle
and his Brothers
for their inspiration and dedication to global education
and social justice for all humanity.

Contents

Foreword

Chuck Denny
Retired CEO, ADC Telecommunications

IT'S MY PLEASURE to introduce this book because, as a retired chief executive of a public company and as a supporter of the Center for Ethical Business Cultures and the Caux Round Table, organizations dedicated to corporate social responsibility, I believe that we can't talk and write enough about why ethical business practice is the key to long-term global prosperity. I think Brother Louis DeThomasis has synthesized important thinking on this topic and has expressed his views in an anecdotal and interesting way to explain why culture and commerce have a better chance of bringing the world together and improving the lot of more people than do organized religion and national governments.

Louis and his coauthor, Minneapolis *Star Tribune* business columnist Neal St. Anthony, have impressive and diverse credentials with which to write this book.

At age twenty-eight, Louis joined the Roman Catholic order of the DeLaSalle Christian Brothers, an order established in France in the seventeenth century to educate the working class and poor. He has been unusually successful in commerce, as an educator, and as president of one of the Midwest's most successful private universities, Saint Mary's University of Minnesota. He has been a corporate board member and confidant to many outstanding and ethical businesspeople.

You may be asking yourself what Brother Louis (a modern-day "monk") and Neal St. Anthony (a newspaper business writer, but not a businessman himself) could possibly have to tell us about business ethics. What could these two unlikely partners, who are actually in the increasingly complex and difficult business world, tell us about the everyday pressures and challenges to act ethically?

First, let me try to capture for you the essence of this man who people affectionately call Brother Louis (pronounced *Louie*). A true story about him that happened in 2003 in far off Ho Chi Minh City (Saigon) may help. At the people's large city market, Brother Louis, physically a portly and balding individual, was startled by the many Vietnamese smiling and affectionately patting him on the stomach as he strolled through the gigantic marketplace. "What was that all about?" he asked his Vietnamese guide and translator. The response was, "With your figure, the people look upon you as the future Buddha. They get much good luck by touching your belly." As an internationally known speaker and writer on issues of business ethics, faith, and finance, it is not uncommon for him to be recognized around the globe. But to be seen as the future leader of an ancient Asian faith was certainly a new twist for Brother Louis.

When you are with Brother Louis, you sense the energy and dynamic of a Buddha or a monk, but with a unique and distinctive difference—he is "in" this world! He does not push away from the world of competing, sometimes devastating, political and economic forces. Rather, to his very core he is a spiritual man who lives, works, and struggles in this world so that the economic systems on this globe can bring about a life of dignity and hopefulness for all. One must wonder how this modern-day monk knows so much about, and cares so much about, wealth, finance, business, and, yes, faith.

A brief look into his past tells the story. In 1914, his father, an immigrant from Italy, came to this country at age sixteen, alone and without money. His dream was the same dream of all those courageous immigrants who came to this country: to build a better life for themselves and their families through dedication and hard work. Brother Louis's father was one of the more successful immigrants, working with passion and determination. His dreams for prosperity and a good life were realized more than he ever imagined possible when he started digging New York subway tunnels as a poor immigrant laborer. His father moved with his wife and three sons to Long Island and began his own sand and gravel aggregate business after World War II. Within a decade he was a major ready-mix concrete supplier, operating four plants dispersed across Long Island, from Nassau to Suffolk counties.

Indeed, he made it "bigtime"! But Brother Louis's father never let such financial and business success interfere with his basic moral principles of living humbly, conducting business ethically, and caring for others with generosity. That was Brother Louis's first and most effective education. He attributes to those lessons his easy and comfortable conviction that faith and finance are not in opposition or a hindrance to each other—if you practice this reality as he learned firsthand from his father.

In 1954, Brother Louis attended a Catholic boarding school on the Great South Bay in Long Island, LaSalle Military Academy. For four years he was greatly influenced by the DeLaSalle Christian Brothers who conducted this prestigious and admired school. Brother Louis says it was from these Brothers that he learned that, with faith and zeal, a person could be successful in the world if he concurrently understands the moral obligation he has to act with a social awareness and responsibility for the poor and marginalized in the world. He was so impressed and touched by the life and work of the Brothers that at age seventeen he wanted to enter the Order. However, his father thought Louis was too young to make such a commitment and "suggested" that he go to college first. And, as Brother Louis says, "In those days you listened and obeyed your parents."

So in 1958 Louis went off to the Edmond A. Walsh School of Foreign Service of Georgetown University. While he was there, he worked part-time as a messenger in a printing company, not because he needed the money, but because he felt restless just studying all the time. In the early 1960s, as Louis was finishing his last year at Georgetown University, he observed that the printing company where he was working had great potential, but was near bankruptcy because of poor management. During this time a new technology called lithography was exploding in the printing world, and new, less-expensive alternatives to traditional printing were available to the entrepreneurs who had imagination. The twenty-one-year old Louis saw that a lithographic duplicating approach to the large, lucrative U.S. Patent Office printing contract could save the government money and make the firm that used this technology higher profits than the traditional way of reproducing patents.

Louis convinced his father and two brothers who were running the ready-mix concrete business that this could be a good investment and would diversify the DeThomasis family business enterprise. Though skeptical, they agreed and backed Louis in his business venture in Washington, D.C. One month after graduating, Louis, the messenger, went to the front office of the firm and bought the firm outright. You can imagine that the owners of the nearly bankrupt firm may have thought they were taking advantage of this young kid.

However, in the first year Louis successfully bid on a very large Patent Office reproduction contract, and, applying his new technology, made a small fortune overnight. Louis became known in Washington, D.C., as an extraordinarily successful young entrepreneur who, though a very tough competitor, was ethical and cared for his employees. Often hiring the handicapped and other problem workers who could not find work at other firms, Louis paid them well and as a result had a very good and loyal work force. He then expanded into an office supply and office furniture firm in Maryland and invested in a Maryland bank. Business was thriving for Louis and his family!

However, in 1967, Louis, now a successful and affluent businessman, answered the call of his spirit to join the DeLaSalle Christian Brothers religious order and leave the business world. When you ask him why he came to that decision, he tells you, "It was really a simple decision. I enjoyed the success and the money, but it wasn't enough for me! I wanted to do more with my life than just accumulate wealth. I felt called to join with the Brothers so that I could teach and learn from them."

In 1968, Louis the entrepreneur became Brother Louis the monk. Naturally, one would think his life of business and entrepreneurship was over and that he lived out his remaining years in a monastery, away from the world of finance and money. However, that was not to be the case. As fate would have it, Brother Louis entered into the life of the Catholic Church just after Vatican II, when there was a mass exodus from the priesthood and religious orders of the Church. Starting in the 1970s, with a shrinking supply of religious men and women, the Church became increasingly dependent on its financial and material resources to continue its noble and effective educational and social mission. However, the Church at that time lacked an understanding and expertise in an entrepreneurial and financial approach to effecting its mission.

Fortuitously, in the ranks of the DeLaSalle Christian Brothers there was Brother Louis. Was this providential or not? Louis responds, "I really don't know, but what I do know is that instead of the life that I thought I left behind, I now was more involved in business than ever before. It was needed, and I had to respond!"

And respond he did. He started speaking out and writing about the need for an ethical capitalism many years before it became fashionable and before the scandals we have witnessed recently. If the business community had heeded his calls in the 70s and 80s, it is possible that the epidemic of deceitful and unethical business leaders wreaking havoc on our economic system could have been significantly reduced. Brother Louis calls himself a "Christian capitalist" because he says he has not seen any economic system that better helps the poor—and that has the potential to do even more—than capitalism working ethically. He is fond of saying, "Business profits when people profit." He truly believes that terrorism and other global problems won't stop until people can live in dignity in a free-enterprise system that responds ethically to real world social challenges.

In 1978, along with a priest and a nun, Louis cofounded the first money-market mutual fund for Catholic organizations, Religious Communities Trust. Their aim was to provide a trustworthy and financially effective cash flow management system to Catholic religious organizations that were either not aware of or could not on their own effectively and productively manage their cash needs. Starting with no assets, this money market trust now manages about $2 billion of assets in an effective and ethically responsible manner.

From that initial cooperative financial success, in 1981 Brother Louis and another DeLaSalle Christian Brother, Brother Joel Damian, FSC, organized and registered with the Securities and Exchange Commission the Christian Brothers Investment Services, Inc.—an investment advisory company specializing in investment management of Church-related organizations. Again starting out with small investments, CBIS now manages assets of more than $4 billion. Its performance record is competitive while investing within the framework of socially responsible investment screens.

Brother Louis is sought after in business circles not only as an authority on ethical business practices, but also in his own right as a knowledgeable and astute investor. During the past two decades, until it was bought out by Bank of America, Brother Louis was a trustee of the Galaxy Funds, proprietary funds of Fleet National Bank, with assets of more than $20 billion. His commitment to capitalism and the free enterprise system, along with his passion and commitment to ethical business practices, and his magnificent sense of humor, makes him a most sought-after speaker, consultant, and director of business and corporations.

Indeed, Brother Louis is much more than a Buddha looking down upon the world from a distance or a monk looking out the window of an enclosed monastic edifice. He truly is a unique blend from the worlds of faith and finance, a person who knows business and knows the values that make life meaningful.

And now he joins with Neal St. Anthony, a respected business journalist who has also worked in financial communications for two public companies, to produce an anecdotal, easy-to-read work on why ethical business that creates opportunity and that fairly shares the profits of its enterprise is the answer to many of the world's problems.

After all, it is only through enlightened capitalists, whether small or large, that we can share our catch with workers and their families and also "teach to fish" so that more may sustain themselves through the dignity of work and fair remuneration.

Preface

IN THIS BOOK we have interviewed several important business leaders to gather their thoughts and experience with business ethics, including Brad Anderson, CEO of Best Buy Co., Inc.; Nicholas Moore, retired global chairman of PricewaterhouseCoopers and CEO of the U.S. firm; Robert (Bob) Kierlin, chairman of the board and past president and CEO of Fastenal Company; Tom Petters, chairman and CEO of Petters Group Worldwide; Warren Staley, CEO of Cargill; Janet Dolan, retired president and CEO of Tennant Company; Paul Meyer, CEO of Clear Channel Outdoor; Brother Michael O'Hern, FSC, president and CEO of Christian Brothers Investment Services (CBIS); and Bob Carlson, former Co-CEO of Reell Precision Manufacturing. Each of these leaders has a unique background, leadership skills, and national and international success, providing distinctive qualities to his or her leadership style and business ethics.

These executives have distinguished themselves in different ways and different fields. They have integrated ethics into their everyday business lives in ways that have helped them to surmount ethical challenges, speak out, recover from adversity, and demonstrate parallel interest with employees, shareholders, customers, and other stakeholders. They have persevered and prospered and demonstrated that ethical behavior contributes to long-term and sustained success for their organizations and the communities in which they reside.

Brad Anderson, CEO of Best Buy Co., Inc., America's largest consumer-electronics and appliance retailer, gained national attention in 2003 when, without fanfare, he decided that he had accumulated enough wealth. Anderson, a millionaire in Best Buy stock, informed his board of directors that any further stock options awarded to him would be diverted to an employee-incentive pool. His decision resulted in several hundred thousand option shares going to hardworking line employees, who have since helped drive Best Buy to record results through 2005. This generous and fair-minded approach, combined with a culture that encourages questions, openness, and transparency in business practices, has helped the company weather setbacks and controversy and succeed in financial performance and customer satisfaction in a tough competitive business. Best Buy has also been recognized nationally as a premier employer and philanthropic community partner. Anderson shares some of the popular and not-so-popular decisions he made concerning ethical issues he faced as CEO of Best Buy—demonstrating that doing ethics is not always easy.

Bob Carlson, an engineer with an Ivy League MBA and recently retired Co-CEO of Reell Precision Manufacturing, learned as a young officer in combat during the Vietnam War that the long-term effectiveness of a leader is rooted in the trust and training of the troops. He found that people would do amazing things against long odds if they were led with integrity and fairness. Carlson, a veteran of several large American corporations, gained national attention among organizations that track corporate ethics when he and other executives of their hard-pressed manufacturing company took pay cuts of up to 20 percent to avoid layoffs and cuts of line employees who made less than $12 per hour during the 2001–02 recession. As a result, the 250-employee company returned to profitability and record performance, including bonuses to all employees, as the economy rebounded in 2002–03. Even today, top executives of Reell limit their salaries to seven times that of the lowest-paid employees. Reell also remains one of the few companies in its industry that continues to manufacture exclusively in America. Bob Carlson's story of leadership in the battlefields of Vietnam and business highlights the importance of trust, sacrifice, and leading by example.

After law school, Janet Dolan began her career as a legal aid lawyer representing people who couldn't afford legal assistance. She brought tremendous listening, learning, and legal skills to Tennant Company, where she rose from staff attorney to chief executive officer until her retirement in early 2006. Dolan demonstrated wise and ethical leadership as she focused employees, the board, and shareholders on the need to put aside short-term gains and invest in next-generation equipment and innovative strategies for the manufacturing of floor- and street-cleaning equipment. The stock price waned as Tennant sacrificed short-term profits, retrained employees for new jobs to avoid layoffs, and focused on high-quality, low-energy equipment that recently helped Tennant hit record profits. She has also been a vocal challenger of the expensive redundancies and bureaucratic excesses of the Sarbanes-Oxley Act of 2002, which has proven burdensome to many well-run companies that never engaged in the corrupt behavior that prompted Congress to pass the legislation in the wake of the corporate scandals of recent years.

Dolan exemplifies the ethical, long-term-oriented leader who is also willing to challenge the system. Her story centers on ethical decision making, and provides an example of a leader who understands the need to sometimes change the rules of the game. Her success shows the long-term gains that can occur when leaders focus on people instead of short-term financial gain.

Bob Kierlin is an engineer and entrepreneur, who founded the Fastenal Company with four partners in 1967. Fastenal today is a global corporation of several thousand employees with a market value of more than $5 billion. Kierlin paid himself a top salary of $130,000 as CEO of one of America's best companies to own. Fastenal has been hailed by the *Wall Street Journal* and many stock analysts as one of America's best-run companies with the lowest-paid executives. A modest fellow, Kierlin believes that ethical business and fair employment practices have attracted the best employees to Fastenal, resulting in low employee turnover, a great reputation for customer care and community service, and a lot of millionaire shareholders. A Peace Corps veteran, Kierlin is in the process of donating much of his wealth to regional educational and community interests. His leadership story provides an example of how giving back often results in getting back the best from everyone, which in turn results in very high personal, social, and financial returns for everyone.

Paul Meyer is the chief executive officer of Clear Channel Outdoor, a division of Clear Channel Communications responsible for outdoor advertising in more than fifty countries. Meyer, an attorney and former clerk to U.S. Supreme Court Justice Earl Warren, has learned to appreciate the cultural differences and nuances of doing business around the globe. By experience he has learned to draw the line at anything that approaches shorting the customer or unfairly enriching local officials. Meyer shares firsthand knowledge of the ethical dilemmas that can occur when ethics clash with cultural differences and the law.

Nick Moore is the retired global chairman and CEO of PricewaterhouseCoopers, a CPA, an attorney, and a director of several companies, including Bechtel Group and Wells Fargo Bank. He recalls dropping clients who he believed were unethical and firing employees who he believed were putting their personal interests ahead of the client and firm. Those decisions were made after long, collaborative discussions with peers and the involved parties, forcing company leaders and managers to examine their consciences and avoid arbitrary decisions made at the top. Moore, a hard-nosed capitalist, discusses his beliefs on business schools and business, stressing the notion of a "moral compass" and the ethical behavior it takes to avoid corporate disasters.

Brother Michael O'Hern, FSC, is the chief executive officer of Christian Brothers Investment Services Inc. of New York City (CBIS), which invests nearly $5 billion in pension, retirement, and other funds for Catholic organizations. His organization, established in 1982, proves that socially responsible investing is a good long-term investment strategy. CBIS consistently avoids investing in companies that make harmful products or mistreat their workers. Brother O'Hern shares why it's important for investors to work with the companies they own to help make them better and more ethical companies. Brother O'Hern's ethical attitude has paid off in solid returns, demonstrating that avoiding scandal and regulatory problems through preventative measures and actively pursing and rewarding ethical behavior are the best long-term investment strategies.

Tom Petters is a hard-charging entrepreneur who went bankrupt twenty years ago, but paid his debts and learned from his mistakes. Today he is known for his globe-spanning entrepreneurship. Petters employs more than thirty-two hundred people and promotes business ethics by giving away millions of dollars to endow international business and ethics programs at major universities. He discusses some of his toughest ethical decisions and how ethical behavior has helped him select the right partners and build a fast-growing retail empire that is known as a tough, fair competitor and a good place to work.

Warren Staley is the chief executive officer of Cargill, the world's largest private company and a leader in the development of nutritional, fuel, and fiber products from crops. Staley, who spent the early part of his career on a Ford Foundation fellowship working with poor people in Columbia, makes the point that his company will never take or make a bribe, which has kept it out of some deals. He says that in the long run Cargill has outperformed competitors who stretched their ethical codes to meet local customs that would be illegal in the United States. Staley, who has led Cargill to record performance since 1997, shares his thoughts on creating a culture of ethics and ethical integrity within the organization.

Acknowledgments

W E ARE MOST GRATEFUL to the many individuals who have helped us during the past year to make this book happen. We choose to use the word *happen* because, even though we wrote these pages, this book would not have become a reality if it were not for so many wonderful, interested, and caring people: people who encouraged us, who guided us, who advised us, and who supported us with their candid and constructively critical advice.

This book would not have been possible if it were not for the generous support and encouragement of Bill and Jean Hendrickson, founders of the Hendrickson Institute for Ethical Leadership at Saint Mary's University of Minnesota. Their unwavering dedication to ethical leadership truly inspired to us to complete this project, especially when the inevitable obstacles appeared that occur in any worthwhile endeavor.

We thank Brother Craig Franz, FSC, PhD, president of Saint Mary's University of Minnesota, for facilitating our use of the many fine resources of the university. We also thank Tim Burchill, executive director of the Hendrickson Institute for Ethical Leadership and his masterful work as our initial editor. Much gratitude, too, for the organizational work, research assistance, and typing of text provided by Sue Hines, assistant to Brother Louis. We also want to thank Susan Omoto for the energy and creativeness she put into promoting and publicizing our book.

We asked several individuals whose opinions we respect with different expertise to read much of the text and to advise us. They were most generous with their time, but more importantly they were most direct and helpful in their observations about our work. We thank the following readers of our draft whose comments helped us revise and clarify much of the text: Bob Ash, chief executive officer, Ebb Services, Inc.; Ron Bosrock, executive director, the Global Institute; Gary Gleason, canon to the Ordinary, Episcopal Diocese of Minnesota; Dr. Daniel J. Maloney, chair of Leadership Studies, School of Education, Marian College; Brother Michael McGinniss, FSC, PhD, president and professor of religion, La Salle University; Loras Sieve, vice president of Corporate and Community Relations, Saint Mary's University of Minnesota; Brother George Van Grieken, FSC, D. Min., director of Vocation Ministry, District of San Francisco.

In addition, we thank the people at Greenleaf Book Group for their invaluable knowledge, expertise, and professional guidance in the publishing of this book.

We are also very grateful to the business executives who took time from their busy and demanding schedules to be interviewed by us. We thank Brad Anderson, CEO of Best Buy; Nicholas Moore, retired global chairman of PricewaterhouseCoopers and CEO of the U.S. firm; Robert (Bob) Kierlin, chairman of the board and past president and CEO of Fastenal Company; Tom Petters, chairman and CEO of Petters Group Worldwide; Warren Staley, CEO of Cargill; Janet Dolan, retired president and CEO of Tennant Company; Paul Meyer, CEO of Clear Channel Outdoor; Brother Michael O'Hern, FSC, president and CEO of Christian Brothers

Investment Services, Inc.; and Bob Carlson, retired CEO of Reell Precision Manufacturing Corporation.

Thank you to all who made this book possible.

DOING

in a SHRINKING WORLD

RIGHT

Introduction

Be good. Be honest. Be fair.
Just simply—Be ethical.

THESE EXHORTATIONS are not something new that people are hearing for the first time. To be something—anything—is not difficult. Essentially, to be good, honest, fair, or ethical depends greatly on how I define that specific quality, how I talk about that specific attribute, or how I tell you how principled I am. Shakespeare's Hamlet was, indeed, a principled man, but his to be or not to be questioning really didn't help much in making him a person who could initiate action—effective action.

In today's global economy, in which actions, or lack thereof, could upset the complex, sophisticated, and interweaving networks of flows of capital and other economic forces, to *be* principled is infinitely less important than to *do* something—the right thing. To *be* connected in the expanding network of information technology simply does not help you or your business, unless you *do* and *act* within that vast infrastructure offering a kaleidoscope array of business possibilities.

Whether it is the businessperson or the business professor, whether it is the employee or the student, whether it is the business leader or the not-for-profit executive, "being principled" just doesn't mean much anymore on this globe. In fact, those so-called principled people more and more seem to be developing into rigid ideologues who claim to have a monopoly on truth—their truth. For the most part, more often than not, these ideologues are causing the problems—not solving them. Therefore, often in this vast, new, interconnected global economy, we hear, "Stop being principled and do what is right!"

"To do what is right"—to *do* ethics—is what this book is about. This presentation explores the underpinnings of how, in the free-enterprise system, corporations can adjust their perspectives and the way they approach their business so that they can achieve a balance between ethics and profits.

The first task undertaken in this work is to briefly summarize a historical overview of the field of ethics so that the reader may better appreciate the difficulty in even defining what is meant by business ethics. The aim of the book is to move a dialogue in the direction of a globally acceptable understanding by developing a pragmatic, effective, and meaningful definition of the term *business ethics*.

An important part of the findings in this presentation was derived from the interviews conducted with several business executives who are truly inspirational in their quest to *do* ethics in their respective organizations. These individuals were clear, honest, and obviously committed to what they saw as their obligation to help coax a meaningful dialogue about business ethics. Their firsthand experiences and insights greatly helped in the development of the ideas in this book. Therefore, the reader will see that toward the end of each chapter there is a section, What The Execs Are Saying, that makes it easy to hear the ideas of these practitioners of business ethics.

In the chapters following chapter 1, we examine the essential ingredients of business ethics that will help organizations balance ethics with profit. The concepts explored are the following:

- There are no simple answers in something as complex as business ethics, so attitude is essential.

- Doing ethics in business requires the dynamic participation of businesspeople who do more than act in accordance with codes and rules.

- Ethical business today inevitably involves an intentional acculturation by business leaders into the diversity of global cultures.

- Business leaders must have the courage to use their imaginations.

- Business leaders must find a new language that will be understood in this increasingly fragmented world.

- Business leaders must believe that if they give more, they will get more back for themselves, for their organizations, and for society.

- Who we educate today will determine the culture of tomorrow's corporations. Universities must remove ethics from their academic silo and fully integrate a pragmatic approach to doing business ethics throughout the curriculum.

Also, at the end of each chapter there is a section we call Take Action Questions. The questions asked do not lend themselves to easy, quick, answers or any one right answer. The answers that each reader comes up with will involve careful thought encompassing the many facets of the situation. Each answer requires actions that need to be taken in order for a solution to be adequate.

Now, we invite the businessperson and the employee, the professor and the student, the not-for-profit executive, the consumer, and anyone involved with religion or church to explore these ideas. Discuss, criticize, innovate, but above all *do*—do ethics!

CHAPTER 1

Just What Is "Business Ethics" Anyway?

BOUT FIFTY YEARS AGO, after many box office successes, the then famous movie actor George Raft was down on his luck. An aggressive reporter cornered him and asked with no small dose of malice: "Mr. Raft, we hear you're not doing so well financially. What happened to the nearly $10 million you earned in your career?" Mr. Raft responded: "Well, I spent some on drinking. Some I spent on womanizing. And some I spent gambling on the horses. The rest I spent foolishly!"

Like George Raft, you choose how to live, spend money, act toward others, and do business largely through the individual perspective you bring to each of these actions. For instance, some business executives with good motivations and intentions for their employees' health could insist that they all arrive to work one hour before starting time and partake in an exercise program sponsored by the firm. Certainly this is a benevolent action on the part of the employer that will help the employees' physical well-being. Indeed, it represents a wonderful perspective on the part of the executive looking out for the good of the employees. But is it ethical to require such a good practice without affording each employee his or her right to choose this "benefit"?

Although an individual's decision making is determined in large part by perspective, it is limited by the law. We know we must always obey the law if we don't want to go to jail or pay fines. Does this mean that as long as we stay within the boundaries of the law that it is okay to conduct business in any way we choose? Does the "free" in "free enterprise" confer on us the freedom to choose our actions?

Just look at any of the current business scandals in the headlines today. In most cases investors and employees alike lost great sums of money because of the actions of key executives in a firm. These accused executives either claim ignorance or present their spin on the law that they claim exonerates them from blame. Though they won't admit it, common sense tells us that their perspective shouts out loudly, "Hey, don't blame me. Though I may have been unethical, I followed the law!"

The law certainly supplies business with specific mandates of what to do or not to do with carefully and precisely defined parameters. After all, that is clearly the role and function of laws and regulations. However, "doing business" is not an exercise or a practice that is easily confined or contained by specific rules and regulations. As we know, good business is entrepreneurial, creative, innovative, anticipatory, and dynamic—always in a state of flux. It can't be completely harnessed by any codes of laws or regulations—no matter how specific. Yet business also can't be unfettered and allow people to do whatever they want according to their perspective.

I guess you can see a dilemma forming. Business needs laws, yet laws can't entirely define how business is conducted. This is why business ethics must come into play as an essential part of doing good business and an indispensable ingredient in the free-enterprise system.

For the most part, business ethics refers to how we decide to act and how we act when conducting business. We say "for the most part" because there exists a limitless variety of perspectives on how to conduct business, how to act ethically in business affairs, and for that matter, whether there even is such a discipline as business ethics.

In his recent bestseller, *There's No Such Thing as "Business" Ethics*, John C. Maxwell contends there is a need for just one principle—one single standard—and that's the Golden Rule. Maxwell believes that while living an ethical life is not always easy, it need not be complicated. Indeed, after reading Maxwell's brief, anecdote-based research, many will feel good and undoubtedly will strive to live by the Golden Rule in their personal and business lives. In the old days of Catholic cultural tradition, Maxwell's book would be classified in the *fervorino* genre: "Read it, feel good, and try to do good!"

While Maxwell's approach may seem like a very straightforward path to living an ethical life, it is not realistic. Once the daily realities of life temper the fervor brought on from reading the book, the fervor evaporates quickly. The challenges still exist, as the complications and complexities of lived reality never fade away. And what is true for our personal lives is also, unfortunately, applicable in the business world. We can be hypnotized by the simple and sincere message of Maxwell's book, but when we reenter the chaotic interlocking networking machinations of the global business dynamics extant in business even on the local level, we are left to wonder whose golden rule provides us with *the* answers we need right now, to help us make immediate decisions.

So we are now left with some difficult situations. Obviously, the law does not and will never be the only ingredient that guarantees businesses in the free-enterprise system will always act honestly and appropriately for their own benefit and concurrently for the benefit of society. Yet business ethics is not the simple solution either, unless free enterprise can agree on some positive and general principles that are acceptable and effective in balancing its need for profits and society's need for business to act honestly. Therefore, at this point it is helpful to explore the development of some concepts in ethics, evolving a contemporary understanding of business ethics that will help the modern free-enterprise system on our shrinking globe to do and to act ethically and legally while conducting business.

A Brief Look into the Past

In this section the presentation of the historical development of various concepts in ethics is like the bold strokes left from a wide paintbrush. The reason for this broad treatment of such a pervasive subject is to present a big picture of a complex dynamic without getting bogged down in the intricate details and nuances that constitute this subject matter. Such a treatment should frame a picture about ethics that makes it clear that this is not a concern modern society "invented" as a result of the notorious recent business scandals; rather we must see that ethical concerns go back thousands of years in the recorded history of all societies and cultures.

You may have limited recall of some tidbits of knowledge and the names of those erudite philosophers who actively sought answers to some of these very same questions. You may be able to recall the Sophists in the fifth century BC in ancient Greece, who embraced the notion that all human judgment is subjective, based on how we perceive reality. They believed that since there can be no full understanding of objective values (values that exist in reality, independent of the human mind), it is one's own perspective that ultimately rules. (Perhaps George Raft was a Sophist!) But less than a century later, Socrates, a fellow you've probably heard of, advanced a counter-argument. Socrates vehemently disagreed with the Sophists, and along with his student Plato, proffered the notion that the basis for acting with virtue (moral excellence), rather than being solely subjective (i.e., acting only in one's best interest), is solidly grounded in knowledge. Socrates and Plato adamantly contended that if people were educated about what constitutes virtue, they would then act with good moral direction. Though this sounds quite nice and even logical, we can see the shortcomings of this theory in a contemporary business world awash in scandals involving unethical business decisions while institutions of higher learning are proliferating course offerings in ethics and business ethics.

Next on the scene was Aristotle (384–322 BC), the pupil of Plato who also tried to shed some light on this question. In his masterful *Nichomachean Ethic* Aristotle voiced his contention that, in the attainment of happiness, avoiding excess and deficiency in one's character and intelligence are the virtues that make it possible to act morally. This is a good lesson. Perhaps someone should have told Ken Lay, Bernie Ebbers, Andrew Fastow, Dennis Kozlowski, and others about avoiding excesses!

Attempts to understand and explain ethics did not end with the death of the last of the ancient Greek philosophers. Throughout the ages, many others have sought to put forth intelligible and effective understandings of the intricacies of ethics: Thomas Aquinas (1225–1274), Thomas Hobbes (1588–1679), David Hume (1711–1776), Immanuel Kant (1724–1804), Jeremy Bentham (1748–1832), Søren Kierkegaard (1813–1855), Bertrand Russell (1872–1970), Charles Stevenson (1908–1979). For more than two and a half millennia, these philosophers and so many more have studied, analyzed, and written extensively on this very subject. Yet, if any of us had the time and the temperament to study the wisdom, insights, and perspective of each of these giants of philosophical history, we would remain frustrated in our efforts and desires to arrive at a clear, agreed-upon understanding of ethics. However, broadly speaking, we could all probably see three distinctively prominent and basic approaches as to how ethics has been explained in a historical context.

SOME BASIC APPROACHES

First, most scholars would identify an ethics of virtue as developed by Aristotle, in which he placed an emphasis on practical wisdom that is best cultivated in a good political community (polis). Ethics was about deriving pleasure from the noble things in life, and deriving happiness through virtuous acts. For Aristotle, ethics resided more in people learning by doing the virtuous rather than by relating rules of conduct. For him, nature was imbued with "purpose" (telos), and moral reasoning involved seeking the purpose within nature as the guiding principle to understanding that which is ethical. Of course, the problem with Aristotle's approach today is that in contemporary society many question if in fact nature is truly imbued with purpose. For many it appears that chaos is more appropriate to understanding nature.

A second approach, promoted extensively by Jeremy Bentham in the eighteenth century, has become known as utilitarianism. His guiding principle was the ethical approach of doing the greatest good for the greatest number of people, with less recognition for people as individuals. For Bentham, doing what is ethically right brings about the greatest pleasure since it is the community that benefits. We see in modern society the natural outcome to this "utility" approach—the cost-benefit analysis. However, we can all recognize that this cost-benefit approach is more conducive to objective, easily measurable outcomes, usually involving money, than the more ennobling outcomes and benefits sought after by the ethically disposed.

A third understanding developed in the history of ethical approaches when Immanuel Kant elaborated on the human rights aspect of ethics. Kant believed there were actions that were not ethically justifiable, even if the observable consequences were good. For Kant, the focus of ethics was not on specific actions; he emphasized people's rights and dignity, developing the idea that persons are an ethical end in and of themselves. These rights for Kant were in fact universal, and furthermore, no one or no authority should impose on the individual person any particular ethical view of the "good" and the "right way" to live. Of course, we can see the shortcomings of this approach. When one uses this standard of individual rights as the sole guide to ethical actions, then the most extreme extension of relativism (the view that ethical truths depend on the individuals who hold them) plays out in human interactions by the lack of any reasonable judgments about the virtuous and the good.

So we can readily see that even with thousands of years of attempts to define a code of ethics understandable and acceptable to all, no one has yet achieved this goal. And while the subject is studied, researched, and analyzed, unethical business practices continue to abound.

For the academic research scholar whose lifework is studying the intellectual nuances of such complex subject matter, the hundreds upon hundreds of serious academic books, monographs, and articles on ethics and business ethics make up a good and appropriate collection of resources. The fundamental concept of what constitutes "good" actions has been dissected by ethicists throughout the ages, as we have just seen. They distinguish the *summum bonum* (the highest good)—because it is inherently and independently good, not because it is a means to an end—from the good that is judged to be good because it conforms to a particular moral standard. That intellectual academic insight clears up *everything*!

Approaching desperation in our search for clarity, we may be tempted to listen to the moral relativists who take into consideration the infinite variety of ethical beliefs and practices of people from different cultures, nations, and societies. In the intellectual milieu of academe, the moral relativists argue that we should not judge which ethical acts, beliefs, and practices are right or wrong. But once again our hopes for resolution are dashed when in our other ear we hear about "absolutism," a theory that holds the completely opposite view, a perspective that moral principles and moral truth are one and that, therefore, universal moral rules exist and must be adhered to. In this brand of moral reasoning, the absolute power of the strong and powerful can (and historically did) dictate and mandate the absolute moral truth (i.e., "mine") to the less powerful through wars and oppression.

Despite our less than satisfactory results to this point, some brave souls among us will opt to forge ahead with conviction and with continued attention to academic treatises on the subject. Those hardy explorers will discover the difference between descriptive and prescriptive ethics, utilitarianism in ethics, normative and meta-ethical approaches, logical positivism, emotivism, intuitionism, determinism, and a few dozen more multisyllabic isms. It is not our intention to denigrate the important and substantive academic studies, approaches, and research that scholars have contributed throughout the ages and that continue today in the ivory towers of academe. This genre of serious academic study must be encouraged more than ever. These in-depth and intricate intellectual gyrations and arguments as to the distinctions of definitions and approaches to ethical behavior in the world today are inestimably meaningful in the academic world. However, they have little meaning in the corporate headquarters of an international company, or for that matter, in the small local business enterprise.

ETHICS AND RELIGION

Surely we can do much better than the dismal fruits of our harvest into the academic world by shifting our attention to finding clarification in the world of religions.

Some argue that no connection exists between ethics and religion. Some believe that even the atheist can act ethically, and that no one need resort to religion as an ethical foundation. Then there are others, Christians, Jews, Muslims, Hindus and other religious people, who argue that religion cannot be separated from ethics. The core tenet for these people is the divine command theory, the general belief that it is the Supreme Being, God, who requires all persons to act justly. Simple, isn't it! God commands, we obey, and therefore, we have behaved ethically.

However, when we choose any religion that professes that ethical behavior derives solely from the doctrine or dogma of that particular religion, we face some daunting problems. For example, different religions—even those that profess the same One God—hold widely divergent interpretations of exactly what God commands. Even within a single particular religion, it can be a fruitless exercise to seek complete consensus on topics such as sexual norms, abortion, "extraordinary" means in sustaining the life of the terminally ill, cloning, and many others. So, where in religion do we find that one clear, unequivocal, undisputed, specific divine command, other than "love," that will cause no disagreement among the faithful? It is clear that even religion is not the undisputed arbiter of all ethical behavior and disseminator of ethical knowledge that will unite all people in agreement on ethical behavior. Even though some level of symbiotic relationship clearly exists between religion and ethics (a relationship even an atheist would acknowledge), a dilemma persists. The twentieth-century British philosopher Anthony Flew pointed to this dilemma by posing a magnificent question: Is conduct right *because* the gods command it, or do the gods *command it* because it is right? Since this question constitutes a classical dilemma, no answer can be given that will satisfy everyone.

ETHICS AND LAW

The law-breaking and ethical transgressions that led to corporate scandals and civil and criminal charges against dozens of American executives resulted in a panicked Congress passing the Sarbanes-Oxley corporate-reform legislation in 2002. Among other things, the act requires more independence and accountability from boards, increases the liabilities for crooked management, and vastly increases the requirements for internal and external auditors. Sarbanes-Oxley also proved that laws and ethics aren't necessarily the same.

In an effort to quickly respond to the loss in public trust created by corporate scandals such as those pertaining to Enron, WorldCom, and Global Crossings, the Sarbanes-Oxley Bill was enacted in less than thirty days. The part of this law that deals with internal and external auditing and testing of systems and controls has proven redundant and financially burdensome, particularly for smaller companies for which report compliance can cost up to several million dollars.

Former Tennant Company CEO Janet Dolan, who heads a subcommittee of a Securities and Exchange Commission–appointed task force on Sarbanes-Oxley, has recommended streamlining some of the so-called Section 404 reporting requirements that many companies and regulators describe as too expensive.

In December 2005, Dolan's subcommittee, after months of research and testimony, recommended exempting small public companies with less than $250 million in sales and $750 million in market capitalization from most of the Section 404 "attestation" requirements, as long as those companies meet certain standards of corporate disclosure and governance. The SEC is considering the recommendations.

Dolan's main point is that even though the purpose of Sarbanes-Oxley is to protect investors and some of the disclosure and accountability provisions are excellent, much of the Section 404 requirements amount to overregulation to the point that the time and expense required are overly burdensome.

"As to preventing fraud, in smaller companies internal controls are much less reliable as a vehicle for preventing fraud than in the larger company," Dolan said, "the reason being that management can much more easily override internal controls. Therefore, other mechanisms are more effective for preventing fraud. These include whistle-blower programs, the presence of independent directors, and other good governance checks on the power of management."

The larger, ethical point is that the remedy for the wrongful and often illegal executive acts that brought down Enron and WorldCom may not be stricter, detailed rules and burdensome, redundant compliance measures that can cost small public companies millions in staff and additional auditing and testing costs. That's called shooting the innocent after the battle is over.

Burdensome regulation will never supplant ethical cultures that encourage discovery and correction of problems within an organization. CEOs such as Dolan preside over cultures that encourage this type of behavior: "If there's a discrepancy, a problem, or something that looks fishy, bring it to the attention of your supervisor. If your supervisor doesn't seem interested or resolve it, and you're still concerned, bring it to his boss. Bring it to a compliance officer. Bring it to a company lawyer. Bring it to the CEO or an outside director, or our 1-800 confidential whistle-blower number.

"You will not be punished for raising what seems to be a questionable or ethical issue in this company. You may be rewarded for it. We want a culture that pursues honesty and excellence on all levels. And we have the chutzpah to encourage our employees to challenge the organization with questions, when they see something wrong."

All companies have problems, and sometimes problem people who do bad things. Fraudulent behavior will always be with us. The sustainable, ethical corporate cultures focus on bringing visibility to questionable issues and practices and resolving them in a candid and credible manner. Bad executives look the other way and put energy into cover-ups if the problems are later disclosed.

What the Execs Are Saying

Janet Dolan, who retired in December 2005 after nearly twenty years as chief executive and general counsel of Tennant Company, believes that business ethics are rooted in a long-term view of what's best for the stakeholders of a company.

It's not about religion, who can make the best case for moral relativism or any other theory, the cult of the CEO, what feels good, what makes the most profit in the short run, or what builds the boss's bank account fastest. "Ethics is all about well-balanced judgment," Dolan said. "You're always balancing countervailing forces. If you're just focused on profit and the stock price as that absolute measure of success, you usually can see two years later the train wreck. And usually it was one thing driving the train—the desire by the CEO to make those quarterly profit numbers and push up the stock price above all else. People get too sucked into very narrow definitions of success. And management will line up for that reward system if you define the culture of a business solely by the quarterly profit.

"If you have leaders who say we have multiple stakeholders to serve, over time they generally make good decisions." That's Dolan's take on what happened at the Enrons, Tycos, and WorldComs a few years ago. The overriding focus of top management, overseen by seemingly oblivious boards of directors, was to maximize short-term profit, the northward push of their stock prices, and the related CEO compensation.

She ticks off the list of names of dominant, dynamic CEOs, now in jail or facing jail time, "who think they're smarter than everybody and those dynamic personalities can spin the reality and say others don't get it. That's what happened and those are corporate demagogues."

Tennant makes street-sweeping equipment and the machines that clean the floors of factories and office buildings. The company's sales and profits were peaking in 2000, along with the U.S. economy, when CEO Dolan and her senior management team briefed Tennant's independent board of directors on a plan to invest heavily in the next generation of more powerful equipment that would consume less time, energy, and water to complete any given job. It would be market-driving, cost-saving, innovative technology. And it would take time and money to bring it to market.

In accepting the plan, management and the board knew the heavy investment would mean some sacrifice of short-term profit to develop industry-leading products that would drive sales and profits northward in a new cycle of prosperity for Tennant.

Tennant's base business was also hurt by the 2001–02 recession, which curbed sales of existing products. And the stock slumped from about $40 per share in 2001 to $30 per share in 2003. In 2001 Tennant also wrestled with a new business-enterprise software that didn't work at first. The company had seemingly moved from a profitable manufacturer at the top of its business cycle to one that was making less money and investing millions in new technology and leaner manufacturing systems, and for a while, as Dolan dutifully reported to her board, a company whose senior management was unsure about its sales and earnings numbers thanks to the new software system. "We went through a baptism of fire, but we kept the board apprised of what was going on, and the board was practical and pragmatic," Dolan said. "That baptism of fire just kind of molds everyone together."

The software snafus were eventually worked out, and by 2003 Tennant was introducing the new, profitable products to interested customers in an improving economy. The improved results and projections moved the stock price from about $30 to a $52 per share close by December of 2005, when Dolan retired as planned after seven years as CEO.

In retrospect, Dolan says that what got the company through the lean times was the manifestation of her management's focus on business ethics: Tennant would sacrifice short-term gain to invest, improve all aspects of its business, retrain people who once worked in administration and areas the company was slimming for new jobs—and resist the impulse to worry about profits during the several quarters when it was transforming its business.

We've seen other companies that failed to invest and sacrificed everything to make quarterly numbers. Remember the since-bankrupt Sunbeam under "Chainsaw Al Dunlop." If short-term profit is the overarching goal, then people will be sacrificed on that altar. That's unethical.

There are occasions, however, in which executives may have to lay off some workers to refocus on profitable businesses that employ more people. These situations are unfortunate, but are understandable and ethical as long as the short-term cost cutting is designed to help the business persevere, grow, and add employees in the long run.

Tennant also passed on potential sales with customers who demanded special treatment or consideration, because these sales would have gone beyond acceptable discounts or treatment available to all customers. "Good ethics is about well-thought-out principles," Dolan said. "When you make exceptions based on economics, the message is clear to everyone in the company. And that can lead to more problems."

The board-approved strategy was spelled out clearly to all constituents, whether investors or employees on the line, who came up with some of the best ideas for improving products and productivity for the global manufacturer.

Tennant, which continued to generate cash from operations even during the lean years, continued to pay a modest dividend to patient stockholders who bought into the strategy that eventually increased the value of their stock by more than 50 percent over the 2003–05 period. Tennant executives, including Dolan, received large bonuses only after the strategy had netted results in the marketplace that started double-digit sales and earnings increases for all the owners of the company.

Dolan widely is regarded as a servant leader, one whose personal prosperity is tied to the fortunes of the entire enterprise. She became a millionaire through her compensation, particularly the value of her appreciated stock in the company—but only as the fortunes of others were rising as well. Most interestingly, she accomplished this in manufacturing, a declining sector in the United States, and in a tough industry under siege from lower-cost foreign competition.

CONCLUSION

There is a story told of Lt. Gen. Chesty Puller when his division was caught in a tight spot during the Korean War. He said to his men, "All right, the enemy is on our left, they are on our right, they are in front of us, and they are right behind us. They won't get away this time!" And so too has it been through the ages involving human ethical behavior. Even though we all speak of ethics, we are always surrounded by different perspectives, situations, philosophies, religious views, customs, and schools of thought. And even though all of these areas can help us pursue a global business ethic, unfortunately they have oftentimes been the enemy. Ordinarily, we speak of ethics as a set of principles involving codes of behavior that explain what is good and moral. However, anyone in business today finds this definition useless and ineffective given the chaotic business environment in which they must operate on a daily, in fact an hourly, basis. Furthermore, in the global setting in which all business operates, there is no consensus about ethical business principles. Yet if we can't collaboratively create some globally accepted understanding of business ethics, then the third millennium economic forces that have the potential to solve the human conditions of poverty, marginalization, and terrorism will never achieve that noble and critically important outcome. In this book, we will attempt to move the dialogue in the direction of a globally acceptable understanding by coming up with a pragmatic, effective, and meaningful definition of the term *business ethics*.

Take Action Questions

1. What determines business ethics in your organization?
2. Can business leaders ensure ethical behavior within their organization if all employees are following the established code of ethics or guiding principles?
3. Is a devoutly religious employee more ethical than an employee who is an atheist?
4. Does virtuous and moral behavior in business constitute ethical behavior?
5. Is it possible for business leaders to maintain ethical behavior and break the law?
6. Do laws and regulations promote ethical behavior in business? Does ethical behavior promote compliance with laws and regulations?

CHAPTER 2

Don t Eat My
Chocolate Chip Cookies

THERE IS A STORY TOLD about a woman who frequently travels to present workshops and seminars relating to religious education that makes an important statement about how we can come to conclusions—incorrectly. We shall call her Jane.

Anyone who travels by air knows all too well the enticing aroma that permeates airport concourses from the mini-bakeries strategically located to maximize sales of their fresh-baked cookies. Frequent fliers also know that these delectable morsels are rather pricey, and in fact, a half-dozen cookies may take a considerable bite out of half a day's wages! Nevertheless, while waiting to board her flight home, as the story goes, Jane succumbed to the temptation, bought six chocolate chip cookies, and looked forward to the guilt-inducing pleasure of enjoying each one of them in the comfort of her own home.

Now her story begins to get interesting. She took her assigned seat on a jumbo jet with four-across seating in the middle of the aircraft. A woman and a young girl (apparently the woman's daughter) sat in the same row, with one empty seat between them and Jane. An hour or so later, at about the midpoint of the flight, the woman nonchalantly placed her hand into the bag of chocolate chip cookies sitting on the empty seat, gave one to her daughter, and kept one for herself. All this time, the woman was looking and smiling at Jane. Jane was infuriated. This woman not only had the pure unmitigated gall to take two of her expensive cookies without permission, but also was so brazen as to smile at her while doing so. As Jane watched the woman eat the cookie, she was tempted to explode at her; but she checked herself and decided to be charitable and say nothing. After all, the cookie aroma *was* wonderfully seductive.

Partly to calm herself and partly because she could no longer resist the call of the chocolate chip cookies, Jane decided that rather than wait to get home and eat the four remaining cookies, she would indulge herself with a cookie on the airplane. While Jane was extracting the cookie from the bag, the woman looked at her with a pleasant smile. And almost at once, the woman took another two cookies for her daughter and herself! This thoroughly enraged Jane, who once again came close to reprimanding the woman; but, with extraordinary restraint, she practiced charity and said nothing. However, she wasted no time in taking the last cookie, lest the woman take that too. And again, as Jane savored the satisfying taste of the last chocolate chip cookie, the woman pleasantly smiled. Finally the plane landed. As Jane drove home, she became intensely aware of her enduring fury over the audacity of the woman to just help herself to *her* expensive chocolate chip cookies. *The nerve of such a person to do that*, Jane thought.

When Jane arrived home, she reached into her pocketbook for her house keys and her hand touched a paper bag. Yes, that paper bag! The bag that held *her* six chocolate chip cookies!

In important ways, this funny little true story (perhaps embellished a bit after being told hundreds of times) represents the not so funny and all too real self-righteous attitude of so many people on our globe. Whether the subject at hand is politics, religion, culture, economic theory, or how to conduct business, the pervasive attitude seems to be that our way is the best way, and we have a "duty" to be self-righteous about advancing and protecting our important and obviously great values that we hold so dear.

THE SELF-RIGHTEOUS ATTITUDE

An attitude of self-righteousness seems to be prevalent in most societies and nations, and in many business enterprises that have achieved at least a modicum of financial and material success. And yet, considering the intimate connection between attitudes and values, there is little discussion of attitude in definitions or explanations concerning ethics in general, or business ethics in particular.

More than ever, because we occupy a shrinking planet and we work within an increasingly vast, integrated, high-speed, and complex global network of business interactions, we must incorporate the element of attitude into any meaningful exploration of business ethics. The worldwide diversity of systems, cultures, and business dynamics compose an enormously complicated context within which we strive to arrive at a basic understanding of the meaning and relevance of today's business ethics.

No effective business ethic is possible today if one's starting point is "my way is the better" or "only" way to do ethics in business. In today's global business environment, if we do not realize that our hands may be (and most likely are) in someone else's bag of chocolate chip cookies, then none of us will ever be able to enjoy those wonderfully tasty morsels. Today, even local businesses—if they are to be economically successful—must embrace a global dimension and participate in the global marketplace. As a result, whether we realize it or not, and whether we admit it or not, our businesses all intersect and commingle with more diverse cultures and diverse values than we can even imagine.

The "our way is the best way" attitude can lead a business to judge that other businesses operate within a set of inferior values. This attitude can, and often does, create a substantial impediment to success, because businesspeople *and* business organizations have pride and self-esteem that make them reticent to do business with any enterprise that views them with disdain or treats them in a patronizing manner.

This raises an interesting and complex question: If we treat others as equal and they don't hold our values, can we do ethical business with them when they conduct themselves contrary to our ethical codes of conduct? How do we resolve this dilemma? The solution is easy, yet difficult: attitude.

In our global society, a sensitive and fearless attitude that embraces differences and ambiguity is an essential element in the definition and essence of business ethics. We can never forget that in business today all of us have our hands in each other's bags of chocolate chip cookies. That's the way it is. That's globalization. That's successful business. And, that's why a modern sense of business ethics must embrace attitude.

Of course, attitude cannot be the solitary component and basis for ethical actions. We are not endorsing the establishment of an ethical relativism in which nothing is subject to judgment or evaluation. Nor are we suggesting that we can or should behave contrary to our ethical standards. But, if we adopt a mature attitude that looks at what appears to be contrary ethical behavior carefully and intelligently, we will be able—with sensitivity and openness—to engage in constructive discussion and dialogue with those who act differently than we do. Sometimes when we explore another's values deeply and without bias, we become aware of a truth that at first evaded us. As

Niels Bohr observed, the opposite of one profound truth is not necessarily an untruth, but rather may be another more profound truth.

SOME REAL BUSINESS SITUATIONS

Attitude is an essential component in any effective modern-day understanding of doing ethics in business. Businesses are not ethical just because they have adopted a code of ethics, although that is often a good first step. But with the kaleidoscopic array of cultural norms, values, and laws that abound in our ever-expanding business universe, codes and laws and regulations are not the essence of business ethics.

Let's apply what we're talking about to the hot topics of outsourcing and China, where our burgeoning commercial and cultural relationships are under fire from all sorts of critics. Although the United States has been sending textile and other manufacturing jobs to Taiwan, South Korea, and China for more than a quarter century, critics—especially in recent years—have been screaming about the ethics of exporting some U.S. jobs to the low-wage environs of these countries, specifically China, a country that politically operates quite differently than we do in the United States, especially in regard to individual freedoms.

So is it wrong that Minnesota-based Donaldson Company employs 2,500 Chinese who earn about $1 per hour in a factory that produces tiny filters for use in computer hard drives manufactured by other companies (hard drives for computers that are completely or partially manufactured in China or another Asian country)? In reality, Asia has essentially become the "third shift" for a lot of U.S. manufacturers. We believe that this is not a bad thing—as long as these jobs take place in safe, clean factories and continue to improve the lives of millions of members of China's emerging working and middle classes.

Firsthand observations indicate that the working conditions in China are improving. The difference is dramatic from the days when the country's millions of peasants subsisted within a poor agrarian economy in which the wealth was commandeered by military dictators and their cronies. That period was followed by a brutal Communist revolution and dictatorship. But now we observe a China that is opening both its economic and its cultural doors to the world.

These changes in China have helped show us how we can learn about the future by looking at the past. Let us, for example, also consider what has transpired in Taiwan and South Korea over the last thirty years. As the United States expanded its commercial and cultural connections with those countries, the standards of living improved for their people, and democracy eventually succeeded military dictatorships. That's indisputable. Thanks in part to their relationships with U.S. manufacturers, Taiwan and South Korea have growing middle and working classes. They have placed more emphasis on educating their people for the workforce, and their press and political systems are now among the most vibrant in Asia.

As their standard of living and their exposure to American freedoms and ideals has increased, those people have demanded not just consumer goods, but also increasingly the rights inherent in a democratic society.

Moreover, to an extent, capital has always followed the lowest-cost manufacturing wages, starting in America with the flight of the clothing manufacturers from New England to the South and, over the last thirty years, to Asia and Central America. It's not always pretty to watch. In fact, it's very difficult to see a factory close. But New England and North Carolina have evolved to higher-wage regions whose economies are more tied to education, medical technology, telecommunications, and advanced agricultural processing.

The movement of some manufacturing jobs from America to Asia in recent years is a continuation of that trend. As in the example of Donaldson and other companies, farming out some commodity-product manufacturing to China can create opportunities for higher-paying development and specialty manufacturing for higher-wage Americans.

Moreover, the preponderance of evidence indicates that the economic recession earlier in this decade is significantly more responsible for most of the U.S. manufacturing job losses in recent years than is outsourcing. And by outsourcing lower-margin work to countries with lower-wage economies, American companies create higher-value jobs in this country in the research, development and manufacture of next-generation products, from processing plants for crop-based alcohol fuels to sophisticated filters that cut emissions from diesel engines and software systems that control manufacturing processes in factories in the United States and around the globe.

Donaldson Company, a global manufacturer of filtration products for everything from truck engines to cameras, employs twenty-five hundred workers in China and about eleven-hundred at its headquarters and flagship plant in Bloomington, Minnesota, according to a 2004 comprehensive report on outsourcing in the Minneapolis *Star Tribune*. But those raw employment numbers do not tell the whole story. Since 1990, the Chinese operation has enabled Donaldson Company to continue manufacturing a product it could no longer produce profitably in the United States. And, during that identical time period, the Chinese initiative has enabled the venerable company to increase Minnesota employment by more than 400 people.

Donaldson's Minnesota-based engineers, chemists, and designers, who earn $50,000 or higher annual salaries, design diesel truck and bus filters that cut pollution emissions in half around the globe. They also design and engineer technologically updated filters for use in computers, MP3 players, and digital video recorders—filters that are produced by the plants in China. Falling disk-drive prices made possible by Chinese production are feeding demand for the gadgets.

In short, Donaldson has been able to move much of its low-value manufacturing of commodity products to China as prices have fallen. In the United States it has grown employment in its engineering and highly skilled manufacturing ranks, which focus on next-generation pollution-control technology products that command a premium price.

So as Donaldson has shifted some of its manufacturing to Asia, where there is also surging demand for some products, it is able to focus on the design, testing, and manufacturing of leading-edge, higher-value products at home.

"If we didn't follow the trend, we'd be out of business," David Timm, general manager of Donaldson's disk-drive and microelectronics unit, told the *Star Tribune* (Mike Myers, Sept. 5, 2004).

Global Insight, an internationally recognized source for accurate worldwide economic and financial data, estimated that 1,854 Minnesota jobs were created as a result of foreign outsourcing in 2003. The firm expects that by 2008 the trend to outsourcing will result in the creation of approximately 6,700 additional new jobs in Minnesota. Global Insight also reports that, within the information technology (IT) sector nationwide, savings generated by global outsourcing led to the net creation of 90,000 IT jobs in the United States in 2003 and should lead to an additional 317,000 jobs in the sector through 2008. Global Insight forecasts 589,000 net new jobs overall for the U.S. economy by 2008 as a result of outsourcing. "For companies in the United States that are looking for growth, they've got to go offshore where the markets are growing faster," Mike Raimondi, a Global Insight economist, told the *Star Tribune*. Donaldson presents an example of how companies can grow from outsourcing and at the same time grow in the United States.

Thomas L. Friedman, Pulitzer Prize–winning foreign affairs columnist for the *New York Times*, says about outsourcing in his bestseller, *The World Is Flat*: "Every law of economics tells us that if we connect all the knowledge pools in the world and promote greater and greater trade and integration, the global pie will grow wider and more complex. And if America, or any other country, nurtures a labor force that is increasingly made up of men and women who are special, specialized, or constantly adapting to higher-value-added jobs, it will grab its slice of that growing pie."

Of course, outsourcing is no fun if it costs you your job. That's a hard reality of capitalism. But the evolution and development of the economy has always caused displacement in the workforce. And observers agree on one characteristic of outsourcing—it's here to stay. It may not necessarily be "right" in the minds of many critics, but it is a reality. Over time it will become more widespread, affecting not only manufacturing, but office and service jobs as well. This is already happening with some U.S. call centers and customer service lines, which have moved to India. Twenty-eight percent of the 252 small, medium, and large Minnesota companies responding to a state government survey in 2004 said they were making goods outside the country in 2003. One-third said they expect to be producing goods offshore by 2008. Thirty-six percent are already importing components for their products, according to the Minnesota Department of Employment and Economic Development. So outsourcing is not limited by any means to huge multinationals like Minnesota-based Cargill and 3M Co.; outsourcing is an economic reality and necessity for businesses of every scope and scale.

Outsourcing is a present and future reality. The challenge is to deploy outsourcing in ways that benefit the most people. It is no fun for someone to see his or her job given to someone in India.

The reality is that an out-of-work former employee will find no consolation in learning that our economy is replacing lower-level jobs with higher-level positions. But this transformation of the economy is a fact.

The ethical business leaders retrain those who lose jobs—or at least provide a fair severance. Unfortunately, the transition to other jobs can be jarring and shake faith in corporate America among dislocated workers. That, too, is a fact. It is unfortunate, and a pox on those executives who permit it. Yet the fact remains that the American unemployment rate of 5 percent is among the lowest in the world.

Our country's commercial, cultural, and political ties with Taiwan and South Korea over the last thirty years led them to move toward increasingly stable democracies, to recognize human rights and freedom of expression, and to improve the quality of their workers' lives as they moved to meet U.S. workplace, environmental, and other standards. A central reason that Wal-Mart's and Target's retail prices are so low is that they both import huge quantities of manufactured clothing and other goods from China, from T-shirts and jeans to appliances and toys. A 2005 *Time* magazine article about Wal-Mart's growing relationship with China noted that only about 10 percent of Wal-Mart's suppliers are Chinese companies, but U.S. companies that supply goods to Wal-Mart have moved manufacturing operations from the United States and elsewhere to China.

Meanwhile, under tough and appropriate pressure from the U.S. government, advocacy groups such as "Sweatshop Watch," and many others, Wal-Mart has implemented high ethical standards for its manufacturers in China without a "holier-than-thou" attitude. To encourage and enforce these standards, Wal-Mart representatives regularly visit and train representatives of more than 6,500 Chinese factories. There are unannounced spot checks. No gifts. No kickbacks. No sweatshops. Workers receive a very fair wage for China and cannot be forced to work more than three hours of overtime daily up to certain monthly maximums. The plants must meet U.S. standards for safety and cleanliness. Even critics agree that Wal-Mart and other U.S. companies are driving the Chinese to implement higher workplace and environmental standards. And it is American companies that are providing the consultation, software, engineering, and environmental services that are accelerating China's emergence from the manufacturing dark ages into a more promising future in which workers have rights and citizens have a right to cleaner air and water.

Andrew Tsuei, managing director for Wal-Mart's global-procurement operations, says that over the years many Chinese factory owners have faked records to show compliance and have coached workers to lie to inspectors. But, in the end, they don't want to face U.S. penalties or the loss of the business of important U.S. customers. Eventually, according to Tsuei, most factory owners come to realize that quality U.S. companies want their workers treated properly, and will not tolerate abuses. "We say these are things we have to have," Tsuei told *Time* (Dorina Elliot and Bill Powell, June 27, 2005).

Wal-Mart is to be commended for its foreign track record. It must be faulted, on the other hand, for failing to provide its U.S. workers with wages and health benefits sufficient to keep thousands of them off public-assistance programs—while its executives make millions. The late founder, Sam Walton, would be ashamed.

It's Not the Law

Traditionally, corruption has been a normal and expected aspect of engaging in business with some Asian countries, including China. While U.S. business practices and laws forbid bribes, kickback concessions, and expensive gifts, many Asians embrace these activities as part of the natural flow of dealing in commerce. We in America will continue to influence the Chinese and other countries through our attitude, behavior, and ethical business cultures because it's the right thing to do, never mind U.S. law. But we don't need to condemn their ways. We need to demonstrate the appropriate attitude by promoting fair business practices and responsible treatment of those who serve American companies in China, rather than by lecturing them about the superiority of our ways. Later in this book, we describe anecdotally how some of our most successful U.S. businesses operate ethically and profitably in Asia and Latin America, sometimes by refusing to cooperate in payments or incentives outside of stated contracts. Companies such as Clear Channel Outdoors and Cargill, when confronted with opportunities or demands, simply refuse to pay bribes to vendors or local government officials. They don't lecture host companies on what is right or better; they simply make clear what is acceptable.

We will not find the solution to our conundrum in legalism and the intricacies of contract law. We're certainly not going to change any business ethics culture overnight just because we abide by the U.S. Foreign Corrupt Practices Act or other government-initiated restraints.

Consider for a moment the unique American cultural penchant for legalisms and signing contracts as the solution to most problems, as the businesslike way to do business. In doing business today, with the ever-present international dimension, we must accept that codes and the law are not the ironclad, definitive, end-discussion remedy for business ethics problems. Why not, you may ask? The law is the law! Everyone understands that. Well, maybe not in the same way. Consider the observation made by Newton Minow, an attorney and a former FCC chairman, in his 1985 study of the legal systems of four European countries ("On the Record," *Time*, March 1985, p. 73). He concluded that in Germany, under the law everything is prohibited except that which is permitted. In France, under the law everything is permitted except that which is prohibited. In the former Soviet Union at that time, he observed that everything is prohibited, including that which is permitted. And in Italy, under the law everything is permitted, especially that which is prohibited!

So with tongue in cheek we could say that given this diversity of perspectives on the law and after extensive research, we have concluded that in today's world of business ethics everything is permitted and/or prohibited, depending on two variables: (1) the last expert business ethicist or lawyer who was consulted, and (2) an individual business executive's proclivity toward prison life. Recognizing that this analysis may leave one a bit perplexed, we offer a clarifying corollary principle: In business ethics everything is always not permitted but never prohibited, depending, of course, on the last expert business ethicist or lawyer who counseled that we empower the powerful with a temperate ethical empowerment. Wow, doesn't that clear up everything!

Unlike Procrustes, the robber from Greek mythology who stretched or cut up people to fit his ideals, all business organizations cannot be coerced, cajoled, or aggressively forced to conform to a code of ethics and to the inherent and inevitable nuances cut deep within that ethical template. What may be self-evident and compulsory in our view of business ethics very likely appears cloudy and innocuous from the perspective of many others.

None of this should lead us to move toward acceptance of the bottomless pit of complete relativism in business ethics, a condition in which there is no inherent merit or value to individual actions. On the contrary, we must endorse the concept that those who desire to do ethics in business today must give prominence and understanding to the role of attitude. Nothing is simple in business ethics anymore. A commitment to do ethics in business today compels us to embrace an attitude that does not fear working in ambiguous and complex environments with others whose values are different from ours, as long as we can expose our convictions before them honestly and sensitively with neither hostility nor self-righteous aggressiveness.

The successful ethical business leader will not fear or shy away from vulnerability, but will openly welcome an opportunity to be exposed to and learn more about the perspectives of others.

The insightful French philosopher Henri de Lubac, in his book, *Further Paradoxes,* offers us a poignant summation of the essential element of attitude as it fits into business ethics: "To differ, even deeply, one from another, is not simply to be enemies: it is simply to be. To recognize and accept one's own differences is not pride. To recognize and accept the difference of others is not weakness. If union has to be, if union offers any meaning at all, it must be union between different people. And it is above all the recognition and acceptance of difference that difference is overcome and union achieved."

WHAT THE EXECS ARE SAYING

Paul Meyer, the CEO of Phoenix-based Clear Channel Outdoor, the world's largest outdoor advertising company, acknowledges that there are different customs and approaches to business around the United States as well as around the world. But he's adamant that it's wrong to take more than your fair share of the cookies. "If you compromise your ethics, you compromise your long-term success," said Meyer, a long-time Clear Channel executive. "We make it very clear that we are not going to cross lines, offer gratuities, or even appear to do anything to influence public officials."

Case in point: Clear Channel Outdoor has successfully bid on public contracts to lease advertising space on buses, kiosks, and bus shelters in Latin America. Yet it has also lost business in some countries because Meyer refuses to pay "excess commissions" to public officials who award contracts.

In one case, Meyer was told a competitor "wired the bid" for a contract in a section of Brazil's largest city, Rio de Janeiro, with some gratuity or bribe to local officials. Clear Channel won the contract—

but only after a successful lawsuit to overturn the city's initial decision not to even open the Clear Channel bid, which was a better deal in terms of payments to the local government.

Also, Meyer has refused to pay advertising agencies that steer client business to Clear Channel billboards more than the 15 percent standard commission on the total cost of an advertising contract. Some agencies were looking for more, without informing clients. "I believe we have business at risk because of this," Meyer said. "But the first time I believe we lose business because we are not 'kicking back' to the agency, we're going straight to the client and laying it out."

In short, Meyer said it's right to get along with people and adhere to local approaches to business, but it's wrong to make concealed payments in any culture.

Nick Moore, the retired CEO of PricewaterhouseCoopers, said he doesn't see "systemic" problems among professions. But ethical breakdowns among individuals who violated the fundamental tenets have resulted in the high-level corruption and failures of the likes of Arthur Andersen, Enron, and WorldCom. Where were the peer reviews, the informed scrutiny of boards, and disclosures to shareholders of what was really going on and who was benefiting?

"Ethical environments are ones that result from the right tone set by the people at the top," Moore said. "You develop a good set of values and you articulate the values. And people hear you articulate the values and then demonstrate that behavior day in and day out. And sometimes it means resigning client engagement or firing profitable, long-term employees.

"If you do things right, you should never be a loner on any issue, including ethical issues," he said. "Heavy consultation is required. I encouraged our partners to assess the character and value systems of the clients we were serving. And we told our people that if you have any inclination that you're not getting the straight scoop . . . the slightest sense that people aren't being candid, or erring by omission or misrepresentation . . . you act on that and resolve any and all issues. You have to have 100 percent faith in the integrity and representation of the client, or you walk."

In short, the executives who have avoided major scandals say ethics must be "baked into" a culture. And line employees must see and believe their bosses are trying to be ethical. Otherwise, good employees will leave and corruption will corrode the organization. That's not good ethics or profitable business in the long term.

Warren Staley, CEO of Cargill, Inc., one of the world's largest privately-held companies, shares Meyer's belief that it's wrong to trumpet a "my way or the highway" approach to sharing cookies or doing business. There are different laws and customs around the globe that pertain to hiring, remuneration, taxes, and other practices.

But to be ethical, U.S. executives must also subscribe to a practical, ethical bottom line. It's just not always as easy to find as the financial bottom line.

Until 1995, a number of policies and guidelines existed at Cargill about how to conduct business. The company formed a "business conduct committee" to consolidate all of these into one source, which was named "Guiding Principles." The Business Conduct Committee then began reviewing and opining on issues related to the guiding principles. The company also publishes and distributes to every employee a book entitled *Guiding Principles* that prescribes general business ethics and practices. Every year, each Cargill employee must review the book and sign a statement that he or she has not violated any laws or Cargill rules—and that they know of no others who have done so. Staley says that once in a while someone may decide not to sign and leave the company.

He also conceded that there are occasionally "rogue employees" in a workforce of 140,000 who may lie or cheat. And Cargill, like other companies, has disciplined several employees and referred others to authorities for cheating in at least one well-documented case within the last decade. "If you don't have processes around your statement of ethics, I don't believe you on ethics," Staley added, detailing the process by which employees are told to consult their supervisors with ethical issues—or seek redress elsewhere in the company if their supervisors don't act on the matter. "We encourage people to 'find a partner' when they have an ethical issue. We encourage them to phone in concerns. We encourage them to go as high up the line as they need to."

CONCLUSION

To define what business ethics should mean today in our competitive, sophisticated, and complex global business world with some pietistic, simple golden rule is clearly not an option. Proponents of such a simplistic solution should be considered guilty of a naiveté that is tantamount to criminal negligence!

So, here we offer the first ingredient for a modern-day understanding of business ethics:

Business ethics is a complex, no-simple-answer activity requiring a sensitive yet fearless attitude that necessarily embraces the differences and ambiguity extant in today's global business environment.

Take Action Questions

1. How can business leaders promote an attitude of excellence and superior quality in a global market when other countries emphasize different values?

2. How can organizations conduct business in countries with cultural norms, values, and laws different from those of the cultural norms, values, and laws of the home organization?

Take Action Questions, continued

3. Is outsourcing to countries with working conditions below the home organization's standards an ethical business practice?

4. Can free-enterprise organizations ever justify doing business with corrupt government officials in countries where people living in substandard conditions would benefit?

5. Is it ever justifiable to break a foreign law to better a situation involving the organization's workers in that country?

CHAPTER 3

You Can't Be Ethical

L UIGI, AN ENTERPRISING AND MISCHIEVOUS poor Italian boy living in Sicily, one day approached his mother with this request: "Mama, I want a new, big, fast bike. Would you buy me one?" His mother responded, "Luigi, caro bambino, I don't have the money." So the despondent Luigi sought refuge before the small Madonna altar in his home and prayed, "Oh, God, please give me a new, big, fast bike, and I will be a very, very, good boy for three months." Later that very day, Luigi's equally mischievous friends told him of their plans to visit the beach in three months to meet all the beautiful girls who would be there. Luigi immediately decided to go with them. That night he remembered his promise to God, so he went back to the altar and prayed: "Oh, God, just a small change—if you give me the new bike I'll be a good boy for two months." The next day another set of friends convinced him to go with them to a different beach in two months' time. That night Luigi returned to the altar with yet another prayer: "Oh God, just another small change—if you can give me the new bike I'll be a good boy for one month." Not surprisingly, the next day a different group of friends convinced Luigi to go with them next month to a different beach to meet the girls. However, something strange happened that night. Luigi went to the altar, looked around to make certain no one was looking, and carefully picked up the Madonna, wrapped it ever so gently in a blanket, and then proceeded to his bedroom where he placed the Madonna under the bed, again making certain that no one was observing his actions. Convinced he was undetected and with the Madonna securely hidden under his bed, he kneeled down at his bedside and once again prayed: "Oh God, if you ever want to see your Mama again . . . !"

Luigi discovered an essential and often overlooked aspect of reality. To *be* a good boy, to *be* anything, is much more elusive than to *do* and to act in real-life situations. While not passing judgment on Luigi's ethical behavior, we can clearly acknowledge that the consequences of his actions are more real than the pietistic intentions he voiced through his prayers.

Similarly, the extraordinary complexity of today's diverse, competitive, global dynamics—and the accompanying cultural, societal, and religious entanglements—are the defining elements not of what it means to *be* a good ethical person, but of the real world environment in which business is done today. The businessperson who fails to appreciate the implications of that reality is on the fast track to extinction. Repeatedly, on both national and international stages, we can observe devotion to individuality, to a plurality of perspectives, and to twisted and evasive legalities as the standards to which business leaders are encouraged to aspire.

Fundamentally, we have always known that we must act efficiently and legally in the conduct of our business in order to create and allocate resources and wealth for the benefit not only of our stockholders, but also for our wider universe of stakeholders. Lately, however, business has increasingly found itself mandated to go beyond efficiency and legality. The cumulative message conveyed by class-action lawsuits, Sarbanes-Oxley legislation, prison terms and fines for executives, and even the dissolution and disappearance of some major companies is this: be ethical in business—or else! But this is a false message. Our mandate is not to *be* ethical, any more than the mandate of a corporation is to *be* business. Rather, in the same way that we *do* business, we must *do* ethics! (Any doubters? Ask Luigi!)

One can't *be* ethical in our pluralistic global business world today. The diversity of people, cultures, religions, and organizations produces so many different moral—or amoral—values and beliefs that the determination of what is ethical is too subjective, too grounded in one's own experiential baggage and societal filters. Attempting to judge the ethics of an individual or a business that exists in a culture with which we are unfamiliar is perilous at best. However, we can *do* ethics!

Ethical Codes—Not Enough

Michael S. Gazzaniga, director of the Center for Cognitive Neuroscience at Dartmouth College, in his insightful book, *The Ethical Brain*, quite successfully makes the leap from neuroscience to neuroethics. In this fascinating study Gazzaniga transcends the quagmire of bioethical quandaries to explore how we make our moral and ethical judgments.

Gazzaniga, one of the United States' preeminent brain scientists, offers an important distinction helpful to our discussion. He asserts that brains are automatic, rule-driven devices. People, on the other hand, are personally responsible agents, which means that we have the ability to regulate ourselves: we are not just automatons, reacting in uniform ways to common sets of stimuli. On the contrary, Gazzaniga sees within people a facility for adapting to what is good, what is beneficial, and what works. He eloquently sums up his solution to the vexing challenges inherent in understanding free will and responsibility when he writes, "The brain is determined, but the person is free."

Most pertinent to our study here are Gazzaniga's perspectives regarding the nature of moral beliefs and the concept of universal ethics. He tackles the essential, haunting, and fundamental question: is there an innate, universalizable human moral sense? Gazzaniga alleges that neuroscience is incapable of discovering a brain correlate for human responsibility, because it is people—not brains—to whom we can ascribe responsibility. He suggests instead that we must look to the theoretical basis of evolutionary psychology to find affirmation that moral reasoning is good for human survival. Gazzaniga—a renowned and accomplished neuroscientist, not a philosopher or an ethicist—concludes that we humans must commit ourselves to the view that a universal ethic is possible. This is possible not in the sense that the automatic, rule-governed brain in each of us is a controlling device that can make us *be* ethical, but in the sense that each of us, through our own personal, responsible acts, can *do* ethics.

With a broad stroke of the paintbrush and with an expansive purview, Gazzaniga's neuroscientific insights can be adapted to our discussion on business ethics. In this sense, we contend that to do ethics means that neither business enterprises nor individuals can simply rely on codes of ethics or accepted sets of standards and practices that will make them be ethical. Though some English teachers may legitimately challenge our forced distinction between being ethical and doing ethics, we stand firm on this point. Codes and standards tend to be viewed legalistically, as constraints, as limits on behavior, as a set or a list of principles. The difference between being ethical and doing ethics is perhaps explained best by these dozen words: We need to stop being principled and just do what is right! There is nothing limiting about doing what is right. In fact, what could be more freeing?

Individual persons within an organization—its executives, leaders, managers, employees—in all their corporate dealings and initiatives, must take actions and embrace decisions that produce ethical outcomes. Business today—for the small, locally owned enterprise as well as the transnational megacorporation—is an incredibly complex, interactive kaleidoscope of financial machinations and multicultural exchanges. Both prospering and challenged businesses find themselves confronted with a quagmire of options: to outsource to another country; to diversify geographically; to engage in currency hedging; to be flexible or rigid in applying work standards to an ever-diversifying workforce.

WHAT'S GOING ON IN SOME BUSINESSES

We've now seen ample evidence that major, respected business organizations in this country conspired against their clients to make an extra buck and further line the pockets of millionaire executives. So much for servant leadership! How about just treating customers right?

Take the case of Marsh & McLennan, headed until October 2004 by CEO Jeff Greenberg, who was effectively ousted by his board in response to aggressive encouragement from New York and federal regulators. In 2003, Marsh & McLennan's sister company, the Putnam Investments unit of Marsh Companies, was forced to apologize, pay many millions of dollars in fines, and settle with investors for allowing portfolio managers at the Boston-based investment company to engage in profitable, short-term trading within several funds in ways forbidden to "ma and pa" investors.

For God's sake! Putnam and the now-sullied mutual fund industry were created for and built around these very same ma and pa investors. Similar illegal and unsavory practices also eventually doomed Strong Investments, where the founder and principal owner himself was the primary culprit. In the first few years of the twenty-first century, these practices reached almost epidemic proportions as regulators pursued sanctions against a number of mutual fund companies complicit in a broad menu of illegal trading activities and practices.

To be clear, these mutual fund villains were not motivated by the potential of doubling their incomes. It was the opportunity to make a buck doing something on the ethical margin. It was often the thrill, not the financial out. Regardless, these were the worst transgressions for fiduciaries in a business devoted to the investment and retirement aspirations of the public.

Similarly, Greenberg's Marsh insurance brokerage—the largest in the world—violated the trust of the very clients who had retained Marsh to seek the most economical and comprehensive insurance coverage available. How did Marsh violate their trust? Try bid rigging and collusion with several insurance underwriters. Some Marsh brokers routinely steered clients to underwriters who paid special fees to Marsh, fees that were often not disclosed to the clients.

This is not a saga about the nebulous rules of doing business in far-off, culturally different lands. Quite the contrary, Marsh and some Marsh competitors (who were also found to be engaged in similar but less egregious illegal practices) make up a substantial element of the cornerstone financial-service businesses in this country. The industry suffered from an infestation of bad ideas and practices from some senior employees who apparently found little to concern themselves with when violating the trust of their customers and clients.

Although Marsh's lawyers argued vociferously about common practices in the industry, the disclosures about Putnam and the Marsh brokerage smelled lousy to Joe Lunchpail, the consumer who ultimately pays the costs for all these "arrangements" through prices of products and services. Once the CEOs of Marsh and Putnam and Strong were dismissed, their successors apologized to the public, to shareholders, and to regulators—and paid huge fines. In Marsh's case, $850 million! But the damage had already been done. The ethical transgressions resulted in lost business, market humiliation for the guilty companies, and the layoff of hundreds of innocent employees.

In Japan, CEOs fall on their swords. But this is America, where these proud men privately admit to having done nothing wrong and where their apologists maintain that the practices that caused their departure from the corner offices did not violate industry standards. And that is true. The apologists are correct. That's the problem. Incrementally, the standards have gotten to a point where they stink.

All these former CEOs hired good lawyers who argued and negotiated fine points of the law and rules that they said were in their favor. Most were not prosecuted.

While they may have escaped the long arm of the law, they—more importantly—failed the basic ethical test: the smell test. The standard they used to judge their own actions was far more lenient, far more permissive, than they would have ever permitted a secretary or a client to use. That's a double standard. It's hypocrisy. It's the prostitution of fiduciary and ethical responsibility. It's powerful individuals not considering answers to these fundamental questions: Is this right for the stakeholders of this organization? Is this something I want to write about in the annual report or tell my mama?

NEEDED: ETHICAL ACTIONS

Traditional academic approaches to business ethics focus on individualistic themes: respect for private property, personal honesty, the sanctity of contracts, employee loyalty, etc. But the complexity of the real world of business today renders this traditional, individualistic approach to business ethics impotent. MBA seminars and workshops have some value, but not as a vehicle for telling people how to do ethics. (How often do we need to repeat the litany of ethical failures: Enron, Arthur Anderson, Tyco, WorldCom, Global Crossings, and so on?)

The old paradigm was to teach businesspeople to be ethical. In the new paradigm of today and tomorrow, we must intellectually and spiritually (not religiously, but spiritually) develop the moral compass of students, of aspiring and emerging business leaders, and even of already established business leaders so that when faced with a range of options they will consistently choose to do ethics, to go beyond principle to do what is right in their business milieu. We must find a way to provide students and businesspeople with the skills, perspective, and commitment to establish a lived ethical framework, a business universe in which individuals and enterprises act ethically within the interdependent dynamics of global economies, markets, societies, and governments.

One may ask, "But what has all this to do with creating a better future for people?" Simply this: Every action we take has an incredible and incalculable effect in the future. If in this present moment we *do* ethics in our dealings with another, our action becomes part of that person—just as an act of greed or self-interest would. Our actions combine with the actions of others to create the fabric of our global society, a fabric that wraps itself around both our own future and the future of others.

If we look around we will find many individuals and business enterprises doing ethics—many more than those who shame themselves and their organizations by acting with excessive self-interest and greed. Yet unfortunately we don't see and read enough in the media about these people who *do* ethics every single day. If we were as eager to expose the many businesspeople who are doing ethics as we are to dwell on the malfeasance of the greedy and self-serving, we would find abundant ammunition for teaching ethics to future and present business leaders.

The foundations of the lived ethical framework we spoke of earlier have already been laid by men like Warren Staley, CEO of Cargill, who does ethics and models ethics in his business enterprise—not by talking, but by doing. And by business leaders like Bob Kierlin of Fastenal and Brad Anderson of Best Buy who go beyond legality as a barometer for acceptable actions and do ethics in all their business actions.

Let's take something Brad Anderson has done since 2003 that cheered employees, encouraged stockholders, and captured national attention. And Best Buy didn't even publicly announce it! Anderson informed his board in 2003 that he planned to donate the allotment of 200,000 stock options that the board had offered him as part of his 2003 compensation package to a pool of stock for line employees. It had a potential value of $7.5 million.

Anderson, who began his career more than thirty years ago as a retail-store employee, had already accrued about $75 million in wealth through his long-term stock holdings by the time the board made the options award. And he earned more than $3 million in salary and bonuses for leading Best Buy to another record year of sales and earnings in 2003. He informed the board in early 2004 that he didn't want more stock options, and that he would donate any additional stock options the board gave him to the employee pool for as long as he remained CEO.

In short, Anderson has decided that he has made enough money at Best Buy. He wants other employees to taste the fruits of long-term ownership and hard work. Best Buy, America's largest consumer electronics retailer, has embarked on a management strategy that puts more responsibility for sales on store personnel.

"If I'm talking about unleashing the power of the people, and I get all the rewards, what I say is rather meaningless," Anderson told us. "Part of what I did with the stock options was symbolic. I'm just trying to do what's appropriate as a leader."

At a time when employee surveys nationally show that two-thirds of the line employees don't trust the "brass," that the compensation gap continues to widen obscenely, and that some CEOs still get paid millions regardless of performance, it's refreshing and inspiring to see someone as prominent and successful as Brad Anderson give something back. Best Buy disclosed Anderson's decision in the fine print of required federal filings in 2004. Best Buy didn't publicize the matter, but Anderson addressed the issue when asked by reporters.

Anderson's action was noted in the financial press and got sensational reviews in the ranks at Best Buy. To be sure, Brad Anderson makes a lot of money. And he is also known as a generous community philanthropist and volunteer. Employees and many customers appreciate that. This is smart, ethical capitalism. Anderson is signaling to the employees and other shareholders that "the sustained growth of this company is a direct result of the collection of passionate employees who greet our customers every day. As a leader, I need to inspire personal greatness and recognize our employees' extraordinary contributions to our company's long-term success."

This is not charity or altruism. And these are not new options that will dilute the holdings of other shareholders. This comes from a person who really understands that doing ethics is good business. Business profits when its people—its employees—also profit.

By the way, Best Buy had record financial results in 2004 and in 2005. Anderson's existing stock holdings are worth even more and several dozen other Best Buy employees who earned those option shares have tens of thousands of dollars of newfound wealth that they can use to buy houses, pay off student loans, and invest in their own retirement.

Brad Anderson's generosity cost him nothing. It earned him higher loyalty and performance from those he is appointed to lead. "The CEO is on a pedestal in an organization," Jon Eisele, one of the managing partners of the accounting firm Deloitte & Touche, told an executive ethics forum in 2004. "The minute a leader is inconsistent with his message, it creates an undertow." Employees generally accept that the boss is going to make much bigger money, but they become a company's biggest detractors when they see big bonuses paid in tough years or new corporate jets acquired when they're told to save paper clips. You cannot fool savvy employees.

Anderson, fifty-six, the son of an inner-city Lutheran minister, built Best Buy along with founder Dick Schulze, another generous and plain-talking, accessible executive. Yet he has also made unpopular-in-the-ranks decisions in recent years to lay off employees and outsource the IT department to consulting firm Accenture. He knows he's got to keep earnings going northward to keep Wall Street happy and the stock price buoyant.

In sum, Anderson says, tough, controversial actions such as these are acceptable if they're done in the long-term interest of building a stronger, larger organization. And those employees whose positions were eliminated were dealt with fairly and generously. Many took positions with Accenture. Anderson said he believed the business case overwhelmingly supported Best Buy getting out of the IT business, hiring a specialist, and growing in areas where it works best: marketing and merchandising consumer electronics. "I was with twenty investment firms this week, and none of them asked about our charitable outreach," Anderson said to underscore the point. "I work for these shareholders. But I think acting in their interest includes charitable outreach. I believe the employees function better knowing they're being treated fairly and they are also part of something bigger . . . that also touches the community."

Anderson is just the tip of the iceberg of fine ethical business leaders who make decisions and analyze their actions by the beneficial consequences for people. His example is an invaluable asset as we seek to educate, inspire, and motivate the next generation of leaders who will do ethics in business.

Another such ethical business leader is Chuck Denny, the retired CEO of ADC Telecommunications. Denny, a former Honeywell executive who took ADC from the brink of bankruptcy in 1970 and helped build it into a company that employs hundreds of well-paid workers and creates hundreds of millions of dollars in shareholder wealth, is one of this country's most community-minded and generous retired business executives, and a vocal critic of executive compensation excess. He has lectured far and wide, using a fast-paced, enlightening presentation essentially distilled from a Harvard Business School study that extols the importance of "followership," the good employees who innovate, streamline, drive revenue, and otherwise get the job done.

Denny talks about how America's most celebrated CEOs often forget that they are carried on the shoulders of their good employees. They need to be wise and charitable stewards of these corporate employees and the corporate capital they deploy.

Perhaps we can add to the ethical framework foundation laid down by Brad Anderson, Chuck Denny, and others by concluding this chapter with "The Ten Commandments of Doing Ethics in Business," guidelines developed in 1995 by Louis DeThomasis in collaboration with William Ammentorp, PhD, a magnificent ethical and innovative educator.

The Ten Commandments for Doing Ethics in Business

    I. Talk the talk of social justice.

    II. Walk the walk of social action.

    III. Put people on the bottom line of corporate calculation.

    IV. Do right yourself; don't leave it to God.

    V. Do what is ethical, and you will do good business.

    VI. Let your work integrate faith and finance.

    VII. Cast aside the symbols of individuality and define yourself by the consequences of your action.

VIII. Recognize that economy, opportunity, and social
justice are the legs on which world society stands.

IX. Give the extravagant gift of your commitment to social
justice.

X. Remember: peace and prosperity in all the
world are created by ethical business practice.

What the Execs Are Saying

Brad Anderson never stole a copy of the Madonna as did our friend
Luigi at the outset of this chapter. But he once was caught in an
ethical conundrum that caused him to do ethics by balancing his
company's code of conduct against Japanese custom in a third way
that works for his Best Buy Company, is legal, and passes the "smell
test." This anecdote and a story from another CEO named Tom
Petters help illuminate our point of how ethics must be practiced to
fit dynamic situations in a sometimes-gray area between what the
rule books say is the black-and-white of ethics.

Anderson remembers getting nervous celebrating a lucrative contract with a Japanese supplier in 1995, as he accepted an
expensive gift at a ceremonial dinner. Anderson was uncomfort-
able because he knew the handcrafted piece was worth thousands of
dollars and violated Best Buy's prohibitions against expensive gifts
from business associates.

"I was sweating profusely," recalled Anderson. "It had my name
on it, and the supplier was tremendously proud of it. And to this
day, I believe it was well intended and not to buy us off or anything
like that. It also very much violated our code of ethics."

Anderson also knew that his executive counterpart from Japan
put a high value on the personal relationship as well as the contractual
one between the Japanese manufacturer and the powerful American
retailer. And he knew that the Japanese liked to commemorate such
events with gifts. But he wasn't expecting a piece of expensive art.

Anderson accepted the gift graciously. He didn't want to insult his hosts. And he knew the gift did not violate U.S. law. "If I had refused the gift it would have been a gross insult to some very fine people," Anderson said. "On the other hand, there were other Best Buy employees standing there watching this." How do you get out of this one?

As discussed earlier in this chapter, a decision may be legal and still not pass a personal or corporate ethics test. Best Buy's policy stressed that executives and others not accept gifts of meaningful value beyond, say, dinner or a show; this gift was worth thousands.

Within a few days of accepting the gift, Anderson was conferring with Best Buy founder and chairman Dick Schulze and others at the company's headquarters in Minneapolis. "Accepting that gift was a dangerous thing to do," Anderson said in 2005. "But I explained my dilemma to the others."

Anderson recommended and the other executives concurred that the appropriate thing to do was for Anderson to make a public gift to charity, and that it be documented.

"It wound up informing our policy, in which I can accept a gift like that as long as I pay the full value of the gift to our Best Buy Children's Charity. That also leaves a public trail that I have accepted the gift . . . and paid for the gift. So that everybody knows that I didn't take any personal gain from that. It's an attempt to solve a personal dilemma.

"We believed it was the right thing to do. We see ourselves as wanting to celebrate the humanness of the interchange. I don't want to prevent that. We give gifts to show affection. I don't want to remove that from the menu."

Conversely, Wal-Mart, a Best Buy competitor, forbids its executives from accepting any gifts from vendors. It's a more black-and-white policy. That, too, is fine.

Anderson and his executives are comfortable with their policy, which discourages gifts, but doesn't forbid them in certain situations—as long as they are disclosed and they are either given away or the Best Buy person pays for them or donates a comparable value to charity in a disclosed manner that complies with company policy.

Tom Petters, the Chairman and CEO of Petters Group Worldwide, the investment company that owns Polaroid, recalls a very disturbing ethical situation about twelve years ago.

Petters, through his closeout business, was attempting to buy millions of dollars' worth of consumer products from a bankrupt company. He was awarded the bid by a bankruptcy court. In order to secure the deal, Petters sought financing for the receivables.

During this time, an employee from a finance company approached Petters and promised to arrange favorable financing terms if Petters paid the employee a $100,000 cash "commission." Petters was torn because this particular deal was critical to his company's growth and profitability. He eventually arranged to borrow the money to pay the "commission" from a Chicago bank.

With the cash in his briefcase, Petters met the employee for the "commission" exchange, but in the end could not go through with it. Petters felt like a cheat. In his mind, he thought, *What would my kids think?* He knew he could not go through with the illicit transaction and told the employee that he could not get the money from the bank. Petters lost the business.

Petters still is troubled by the transaction because in the end he lied to get out of the deal. "My briefcase full of cash was under my chair. He told me that I didn't understand how business works." But Petters does understand. His company has done dozens of closeout sales. And he has paid real, explicit commissions to financiers and others for explicitly disclosed contractual work. He's not proud of how he handled that particular situation and the lack of communication, but he didn't pay a bribe. That's the bottom line. Petters is a better, far more successful businessman for admitting and learning from his mistakes.

"We take our ethics with us wherever we go to do business," Petters said. "Reputations cannot be bought and sold. Ethics means everything to me. It's the beginning of every relationship and continues as a 'must have.' I'd rather do a lousy deal with some guy I trust than a great deal with a guy I don't trust. Your chances of coming out ahead on the deal are far better. You don't have to deal with the devil."

In 2004, Tom Petters's college student son John was killed in a tragic accident in Italy. John was a student at Miami University of Ohio. He was an ethical young man and a business student. Later that year, Tom Petters donated $10 million to build the John T. Petters Center for Ethical Leadership and Professional Skill Development on the Miami campus. It strives for a unique environment that creates interdependent and collaborative work to promote scholarship and incorporate research and best practices into the curriculum while teaching skill development in the area of ethics.

Clearly, Anderson and Petters know that not every ethical situation is described in law or a rule book. But every gray-area ethical situation must be disclosed, discussed, and acted on in a good faith that can be explained to all stakeholders.

CONCLUSION

No longer can we be content to accept business ethics as some state of being in conformity to certain codes, principles, or values in and of itself. If business ethics is to have any meaning in a global society, it will not be manifested by what we preach, but rather by what we do. We must go beyond principle and do what is right in order to effectively communicate anything meaningful about business ethics at all.

Here is the second ingredient for a modern-day understanding of business ethics:

Business ethics is practiced by businesspeople who, by consistent and dynamic participation in responsible acts, do ethics and inspire others to do the same. They know, understand, impart to others, and act on the premise that doing ethics requires more than acting in accordance with some prescribed code or set of rules.

Take Action Questions

1. As a small but profitable firm, you are economically unable to fully execute all the compliance issues involved with Sarbanes-Oxley legislation. Do you find ways to circumvent some provisions if you are confident that such lapses will go undetected?

2. How can leaders motivate executives and managers to work effectively with employees they perceive to be dishonest and feel no obligation to treat fairly?

3. As a sales manager, you see that your top-producing salespeople, though technically following your published code of ethics, are treating customers unfairly. What approach should be taken to maintain sales and ethical practices?

4. How can a business leader change an organization from being principled to just doing what is right?

5. How can business leaders convince an organization's board of directors that acting ethically results in success and profitability?

CHAPTER 4

From This Cup
They Drank Their Life

T HOUGH RUTH BENEDICT WROTE *Patterns of Culture* in 1934, her classic study of three primitive cultures stands as an incredibly insightful commentary on our times and casts a pertinent light on current-day global dynamics. Perhaps her most illustrative conceptualization of the critical importance of understanding the role of culture in societies, if one is to understand how to live in our modern era, is her use of a proverb from the Digger Indians. A chief of the Digger Indians said to her one day, "In the beginning God gave to every people a cup, a cup of clay, and from this cup they drank their life. They all dipped in the water," he continued, "but their cups were different."

Ruth Benedict understood that the imagery expressed by this simple, humble man brought to focus something that had value equal to life itself, the whole fabric of his people's standards and beliefs. She reflected on the reality that this man had straddled two cultures—ancient and modern—whose values and ways of thought were so different, or to use her word "incommensurable." Then she realized that in Western civilization, in general, our experiences have been quite different. Benedict observed that we are bred to one cosmopolitan culture, a culture in which we are not sensitive, either socially or psychologically, to other cultures.

No wonder nations and religions have warred with each other ad infinitum, each claiming in their own way that they had a just cause and sometimes God on their side. We don't need the Crusades of the past to fall back on. For years, the British tried to rule Iraq and other Middle Eastern states—even to the point of being in conflict with France and Germany. They all wanted to control Iraq's oil. Today, the United States effectively controls Iraq, although a viciously effective coalition of minority Muslims, fighters from neighboring Arab states, and others have waged an effective and murderous war of car bombs and sabotage to keep us from pumping the oil, enforcing the peace, and effecting the democratic transition that President George W. Bush predicted in early 2003.

In fact, history proves that, for better or worse, Iraq ultimately will be for Iraqis, Afghanistan will be for Afghanis, and Vietnam will be for the Vietnamese. Ironically, thirty years ago, American soldiers were fighting in Vietnam to keep the nationalist Ho Chi Minh from sweeping his country from the north with a unifying and communist government supported by China and Russia. After ten years of fighting, America grew weary and left. The corrupt South Vietnamese government fell to the Communists in 1975. Over the course of a generation, Vietnam warred with China and Cambodia—adjacent Communist countries with which it long has had conflict—evidence that dogma and ideology don't trump nationalism. Eventually Vietnam started to loosen its laws, liberalized trade, and lo and behold, U.S. veterans of the Vietnam War in the Senate, in the State Department, and in industry worked with the Vietnamese government to encourage cultural and commercial ties with the United States that are beginning to flourish.

Dave Roberts, a former combat Marine in Vietnam who is now the chief executive of factory-equipment manufacturer Graco, Inc., shakes his head in disbelief over how a place where he once fought is now a place where the children of his former adversaries run modern plants that meet U.S. environmental standards and use Graco paint sprayers.

Similarly, Paul Smallwood, a suburban Minneapolis engineer who emigrated from Vietnam as a teenager, runs a small company that has a booming business in environmental engineering consulting for the Vietnamese and regularly hosts Vietnamese in this country who are interested in our commerce and culture.

We are different countries. But commerce, culture, the pursuit of a better standard of living, environmentalism, and education are things that inspire dialogue, negotiations, joint ventures, and ultimately a commonality of interests and shared perspectives. Our avowed national enemies can become our own product suppliers and business partners, and even the classmates of our children through study abroad programs. Though it's often a messy process, it beats war any day.

The conduct of business today is affected by a wide array of diverse cultural forces. We cannot deny the presence of the notorious unethical, greedy miscreants so widely publicized in the media. However, the vast majority of businesspeople honestly and caringly embrace the current competing culture issues and welcome the challenges inherent in dealing with the seemingly unsolvable cultural issues that present themselves daily in our increasingly globalized business milieu. Our attention should shift to these business leaders, whom we must respect and support in their attempts to do ethics so that their enterprises, their stakeholders, and global society all benefit.

The global economy that we all talk about today is not something new. It didn't come about just in these past few decades. Throughout most of history, the global dimension and its concurrent cultural complications for business have always been there. It didn't start with Vietnam and Iraq. Just look back in history. If we could interview Marco Polo, Alexander the Great, Charlemagne, or those leaders during the late nineteenth and early twentieth centuries in the former British Empire, would we be able to cope better with the global economic business challenges of today? The answer: probably not!

In the global economic enterprises of today, distance is no longer the factor that it was in the past. Frances Cairncross, senior editor at *The Economist*, captured this fact in the title of her 1997 book, *The Death of Distance*. An enormous new dimension with both qualitative and quantitative implications has become part of the fundamental global business enterprise equation. That dimension, of course, is the new "transport system," the electronic and technological innovations in communications. The "death of distance" has created an instantaneous communications network of complex interactions that make doing business not only qualitatively, but also quantitatively different. These technological innovations have not only brought about a dramatic change in doing business, they have also transformed doing ethics.

What do we mean when we say "global economics"? We refer to the cultural complex of diverse forces—economic, political, societal, religious, and ethical—a cultural complex that requires every free-enterprise organization to transform itself to its very core, even to the interpretation of its mission, if it is to experience success in today's global business environment, where understanding and accommodation of different values is a necessity. Ruth Benedict chose the perfect word to explain this dynamic of straddling cultures; it is, indeed, "incommensurable," there is nothing to compare it to.

Today's new global economic society is no longer situated in physical geography within a definitive space; rather our new interactive, connected, intertwining, instantaneously present technological reality is in spiritual geography. Not religious geography, but spiritual geography, in the sense that our global economic reality exists more in minds, values, and the Internet's cyberspace of portals than in any one geographical port. As a result, the dynamics that we must utilize to reach our customers are no longer ships to get our products to ports, but culture to help us traverse the many, varied portals of economic systems, practices, and values. Truly, incommensurable!

Let us consider Cargill, the international conglomerate that once generated much of its income as a secretive commodities trader. A generation ago, through its own telecommunications-and-computer network, Cargill's weather-and-trade experts took advantage of everything from inclement weather to geopolitical tensions to cease market gyrations for seed, fertilizer, and food and produce better profits for the company.

Today, information is readily available; no individual or company can control or limit the flow of information. Cargill has transformed itself into a nutrition company that increasingly focuses its resources on developing crops that require less fertilizer and energy, on producing fuels from crops, on extracting value-added medicinal and nutritional supplements from increasingly versatile and valuable corn and soybean crops, and even on converting corn resin into synthetic and plastic fabrics that were formerly made from oil-based products.

Cargill produces millions of barrels of corn- and soy-based fuels annually that replace increasingly expensive foreign oil. And companies such as Cargill are on the cusp of breakthrough technology that will convert cellulose—not just in the corn kernel, but also in the so-called agricultural wastes of corn stalks and husks and other farm byproducts—to usable fuels, thus increasing greatly the output and efficiencies of the giant alcohol refineries being built by Cargill and many farmer-owned cooperatives.

Cargill is a leading-edge pioneer in the development of cleaner renewable fuels. Its success bodes well for the United States and world economies for many reasons. It will enhance our national security. The successful development of alternative fuels may also cause the Middle Eastern despots, to whom we are now so beholden, to increasingly democratize their cultures and open up their economies. If we have substitute fuels, human rights and fair trade—not oil—will drive our foreign policy, as they should.

Good, ethical competition can breed improved relationships and advance capitalism, wealth creation, and higher living standards. But the consequences of good ethical competition and business practices extend beyond economic considerations; in fact, ethical, competitive business can be a more effective driver of human rights and political change than war.

Above all, we must be respectful and understanding of other cultures. We must learn to tolerate—and, in many cases, even embrace—differences without ever giving ground on the basic and fundamental international principals of the rights to freedom, food, and health.

A well-respected practitioner of these values is Cargill CEO Warren Staley, an executive who speaks two languages and who, as a young man, worked for a development bank in Colombia. Staley spent more than a decade living in Latin America and Europe. He believes and insists that Cargill managers and workers in other countries are the leaders of the company on the ground. From China to Chile, Cargill workers enjoy fair pay; receive educational and health care benefits; and work in safe, clean factories. And local Cargill employees control decisions on the investment of in-country profits for community-development programs and projects.

We would all do well to emulate Warren Staley and the corporate culture of Cargill by setting a gold standard in our organizations that is sensitive to and embraced by the local people. When we do that, we raise standards for all. That's the model.

Therefore, a profound understanding of the place of culture in today's economic reality is the ultimate phenomenon with which we must deal. Of course, there are many, many definitions of culture. A review of the writings of anthropologists and other experts on culture would probably surface these ideas:

- A meaning system by which people define themselves
- A belief system
- A carrier of people's values
- A basic set of assumptions that explain reality
- An integrated system of learned behavior
- Religious practices
- Political practices
- Economic activities

Each individual is a creature of culture; and yet, culture is not totally comprehensible since it is a variable system that is neither fixed nor static. With an understanding of this context, the Digger Indian proverb makes sense: "God gave to every people a cup, a cup of clay, and from this cup they drank their life. They all dipped in the well, but their cups were different."

Yes, we are all dipping into the same water, the one global economic reality; yet we have our different cups, our own unique cultures. This is the predicament of doing business in the new global society. Within the Digger Indian proverb, we can find not only the enormous challenges to do business, but also the daunting hurdles we face to do ethics.

Many businesspeople find these challenges intimidating. In his fascinating book, *Beyond Culture*, Edward T. Hall, renowned as one of the most original anthropologists of our era, stresses this point.

He contends that if we are to come to grips with these deep cultural divides and differences, they must first be recognized, made explicit, and embraced as a prerequisite to arriving at some "universalizable" underpinning of our human nature. In essence, Hall says that we must transcend our own culture, both the overt, obvious culture, and the unconscious and less visible culture.

Hall is quite explicit in his indictment of the West and our delusory conviction that we have a corner on reality, what he terms our perceived "pipeline to God." Infected with that perspective, we are inclined to view other cultures as realities that are distortions or inferior systems of thought. Hall is quick to point out that we are not alone in this attitude. Most other cultures also are convinced of the superiority of their systems and beliefs.

All of this reinforces the issue raised in chapter 2 as to the vital role of attitude when it comes to doing ethics in business; however, our point here regarding cultures is that until we examine, study, and comprehend cultural systems, including our very own, we cannot expect businesspeople to practice ethical behavior effectively in a global economy—or, for that matter, even to do successful business. All this continues to support the dilemma thrust upon global business, namely the ambiguity inherent in comprehending the diversity in the patterns of cultures extant.

In his book, *Moral Courage,* Rushworth Kidder, PhD, founder of the Institute for Global Ethics, quotes Vaclav Havel, former president of the Czech Republic, on the necessity of discovering and building on universalizable values: "If humanity is to survive and avoid new catastrophes, then the global political order has to be accompanied by a sincere and mutual respect among the various spheres of civilization, culture, nations, or continents, and by honest efforts on their part to seek and find the values or basic moral imperatives they have in common."

WHAT THE EXECS ARE SAYING

Warren Staley, the Spanish-speaking chief executive of Cargill, one of America's farthest-reaching food companies, has lived and worked in Latin America and Europe for much of his career. Cargill's success is rooted in acculturation, hiring and promoting local employees, and acceptance by host cultures and communities. Local Cargill workers from Honduras to Japan have input, in concert with regional management about how the company should operate and invest, including philanthropically. To be successful in Argentina, for example, Staley knows that Cargill must operate like a local company that benefits the host country. It's part of sensitivity to local customs. But that sensitivity goes only so far.

Staley also learned early in his career that there are local customs officials and others around the globe who know how to ask for a bribe in the course of doing business with U.S. and other foreign companies. These also are unethical and bad business practices, he concluded in 1973 when he was in charge of Cargill's Argentina business. Cargill was operating what was becoming a very profitable soybean processing plant when a critical piece of equipment arrived in the port.

Staley's plant management had already ordered the critical equipment needed to bring the plant to peak operations when Staley was told by a subordinate that there would be an additional charge on top of the cost of buying and ordering the part to be delivered. A local customs agent wanted $15, a small but customary markup that he was told supplemented the meager salaries of Argentinean customs agents.

Staley consulted his boss in the States, and they decided the request was a bribe. Cargill didn't pay bribes, regardless of how customary the practice was in the local country.

"We shut down the plant," Staley recalled. "It was very expensive every day we were down. Over a $15 bribe! It wasn't called a bribe, but we knew it was a bribe. If we had paid, I don't think I could have looked my employees in the eye. It was not a good economic decision, but it was a big issue. I told the Cargill people that if it starts at just a few pesos, pretty soon it's more pesos and pretty soon it is $1 million. But if you say no, pretty soon, they'll go pick on somebody other than Cargill."

That's what happened in that case—and in most where small bribes are not written into law but are part of the culture, from Latin America to Malaysia to China.

Staley consented to a one-hour interview on ethics for this book. Yet the CEO of America's largest private company and one of its widest-ranging global citizens spent more than two hours talking about the importance of being adaptable to local rules and customs—without breaking down when it comes to the linchpins of doing ethics.

Staley recalled a situation in the interior of China in which a $150 million state-of-the art processing plant was delayed because Cargill refused to pay a gratuity to an inspector as part of an environmental permitting process. "You can go to the central government and they look at you like you are crazy," he recalled. "You have to go back to the local official and say, 'We're not paying you.' Eventually they go away. That happens to us every day somewhere in the world. Eventually, they understand we simply do not operate that way and apparently leave to find more willing participants."

Staley acknowledges that not every Cargill manager has always lived up the Cargill code and that competitors sometimes pay small "commissions" to get things done faster in countries where it is customary. "I can give you examples of where good ethics may not be good business in the short term," said Staley, an engineer with small town, working-class roots who joined Cargill in 1969 after working under a Ford Foundation grant in Columbia for two years helping working-poor entrepreneurs. "But good ethics is good business in the long-term. And if we can't see a good business model in a country using our ethical standards, we won't do it. And if employees see you paying bribes, I guarantee they will start stealing from the company."

CONCLUSION

To do ethics in today's global business environment, business leaders must be reasonably acculturated into many cultures, societies, and mores. Never should we think that ethical business decisions are simple, straightforward dictums in today's environment. We become better and more articulate business leaders when we pursue more knowledge about our own culture, and when we seek knowledge of other cultures, we indicate our appreciation of the people in those cultures and we encourage them to exercise the freedom to be themselves. Or, as Edward Hall poignantly expressed in *Beyond Culture*, "Self-awareness and cultural awareness are inseparable, which means that transcending unconscious culture cannot be accomplished without some degree of self-awareness. Used properly, intercultural experiences can be a tremendous eye opener, providing a view of one's self seldom seen under normal conditions at home."

As we continue to expand the ingredients of our understanding of modern-day business ethics, we place this into the mix:

Business ethics involves intentional and comprehensive study by business leaders to acculturate themselves and their enterprises into the diversity of global cultures. They do this not only to acquire knowledge of others, but also to seek self-awareness.

Ultimately, business ethics can only be effective in today's global society to the degree that business leaders can see and understand that the diversity in the patterns of culture must be harnessed, not only so people can do business together, but also so people may work together for the benefit of everyone (i.e., doing ethics). Or, as Hall states so eloquently, "Until we can allow others to be themselves, and ourselves to be free, it is impossible to truly love another human being; neurotic and dependent love is perhaps possible, but not genuine love, which can be generated only in the self."

Take Action Questions

1. You are the CEO of a large firm in the West and support the religious traditions of your culture and how you do business. Should you attempt to operate your business in a country with very little political freedom and atheistic values?

2. You are an American manager of a subsidiary of your firm in China. Do you follow the customs and ways of the Chinese or of the United States when there is a conflict of values present?

3. As a CEO of an international conglomerate operating in many different countries, how do you effectively communicate consistent core values within such a diversity of cultures?

4. When attempting to start to expand a business in another country, do you start by explaining your values and principles?

5. Since the United States is the most powerful economic force in the global economy, does it stand to reason that the States' way of doing business must become *the* way to do business everywhere?

CHAPTER 5

Who Would Have Disagreed with Aristotle?

J
UST A FEW MILLENNIA AGO Aristotle believed that the
heavier an object, the faster it would fall to the ground. And
who would have disagreed with Aristotle, the greatest thinker
of his time? All it would have taken to see that Aristotle was abso-
lutely wrong was to take a heavy object and a lighter object, drop
both from the same height, and see what happened. Why didn't
Aristotle think of that?

As unbelievable as it may be now for our modern, scientific
minds, it took about two thousand years before someone—Galileo,
in 1589—thought to drop both objects and observe. Galileo gathered the cognoscenti of his time to the Leaning Tower of Pisa, and
simultaneously pushed off a ten-pound weight and a one-pound
weight for everyone gathered to see what would happen. Everyone
there—every single person—saw that both weights landed on the
ground at precisely the same time. Yet, incredibly, history records

that all of those learned observers flatly denied what they saw. They continued to believe the "truth" that Aristotle was right and Galileo wrong. Indeed, the power of belief in conventional "wisdom" was intact!

Even though Galileo's conclusion was not accepted, we do know that his spirit of scientific inquiry began to flourish during the Renaissance, in particular the sixteenth century, with its abiding interest in humanism and intense curiosity in the phenomena of nature.

Two centuries later, in eighteenth-century Europe, the Philosophie des Lumières went even further in opposing traditional beliefs in authority, doctrines, and values, and replaced them with the Enlightenment, or the "light of reason," what Immanuel Kant characterized as humankind's emergence from its self-inflicted tutelage. That emerging milieu planted the seeds for the growth of verdant pastures and abundant harvests of technological transformation: the steam engine, the radio, the airplane, the television, and the computer. Each, in its own way and interconnected with other technologies, exponentially changed its contemporaneous world and, of course, all the worlds that followed.

This persistent evolution has imprinted itself on our intellectual approaches to economic and business thinking and decision making. We want the facts, all the empirical data that can be spewed out of our computers. We now rely on charts, graphs, numbers, ratios, returns on investments, financial models, currencies, and so on. We employ high-powered Texas Instruments calculators and Dell computers powered by Intel Pentium processors to run our projections. We tap the seemingly infinite capacity of the Internet to find competitor and market intelligence and to find markets, opportunities, and the most advantageous sites for factories and distribution centers around the globe. We are awash in facts that range from land and labor costs to local laws and regulations. We have in our possession facts, facts, and competing facts in unprecedented amounts.

But are the facts factual? Are they valuable? Do they help us make good decisions? Isn't it true that we can cause statistics to tell different stories and lead to different conclusions depending on how those statistics are used and displayed?

The truth is that facts, like culture, are evolving. Clifford Gertz, a prominent and influential anthropologist, has studied the phenomenon called "facts." In his book, *After the Fact*, he suggests that in the currently evolving post-structuralist, postmodernist, posthumanist age, there is no longer one prevailing standard for judging what the facts are; nor, indeed, even for what a fact is. Just as happened in our discussion of the effects of culture on the global society and global economics, Gertz's insight leads us to a conundrum. Are we to admit that our knowledge base can no longer demonstrate scientific truth or provide us incontrovertible economic facts? Are we to be content with a cacophony of chaotic statistics, matrices, and numbers and let the economists continue to present their "expert" explanations and models? Also, what does this say to us about making ethical business decisions—or more precisely, is it even possible to make any meaningful ethical business decision in this foggy environment?

There is a path out of this quagmire that should be explored and taken if we are to do business successfully and do ethics in our evolving global world economy. More than at any time in the history of humankind, the role of imagination is critical. Imagination is the new capital essential for investment in the emerging global economy of the third millennium.

It Takes Imagination

In her novel *Beloved*, Pulitzer Prize winner Toni Morrison tells the story of an African-American woman slave who was a preacher to her companion slaves. Her name was Baby Suggs. Preacher Suggs would secretly meet with her congregation of fellow slaves on

Saturday afternoons. She would take her congregation deep into the woods in a small open field so as to be undetected by the master. Baby Suggs had a dazzling influence on her "parishioners." At times, they were crying from her heartfelt sermons, while at other times she would have them laughing and dancing. Surprisingly, Baby Suggs never gave sermons in which she preached of fire and brimstone, or sin and hell. She never preached to these oppressed souls—these captive and broken bodies before her—the usual expected pious exhortations on the lips of the ordinary preachers. Never. Instead Baby Suggs told her congregation of slaves that the only grace they could have was the grace that they could imagine. *If they could not see it, they would not have it!*

The global economy today, with its multiple webs of interactions, cultural diversity, complexities, and interdependence requires an imagination that will help the business leaders of today to see, think, and solve problems in a different way. Imagination will help those leaders to see things that are not apparent in the statistics, numbers, or charts. Imagination must not be seen as the enemy of the data-driven, factual economic reality, but rather as a creative and dynamic ingredient to help leaders understand and see the real, the good, the helpful, and the profitable in today's global economic mix.

It's the kind of imagination that a generation ago empowered Bill Gates and his band of college contrarians and doubters of the conventional thinking to take existing computer electronics and leapfrog to a new software called Microsoft. By putting computing power literally in the hands of thousands of creative managers, entrepreneurs, writers, and planners, Microsoft helped individuals and organizations unleash tremendous creativity and productivity.

Microsoft's soaring stock price also made Gates rich, as well as hundreds of Microsoft employee-owners and other shareholders. Much of their winnings went into new businesses that employ thousands. And Gates spearheaded a Microsoft charitable surge that put millions into fighting AIDS and promoting health in the developing world. This is profit with purpose—investing excess into new business and to aid the least fortunate among us!

In order to have successful and profitable enterprises tomorrow, today's business leaders must expand the power of their imaginations. The reason for this is simple, though illusive. In today's global economic dynamic, there is a growing pervasive disconnect with the traditional paradigm of relying solely on our comfortable Western traditions. No longer are we able to analyze economic reality through rational, scientific, direct, dualistic, and linear logic. Those who aspire to success as business leaders must be shrewd and uniquely observant to see something, quietly but persistently, changing in this vast essential analysis. Linda J. Shepherd, in her book, *Lifting the Veil: The Feminine Face of Science*, describes an evolving process, fuzzy logic. Shepherd borrows this concept from its originator, Professor Lotfi Zadeh of the University of California at Berkeley. Fuzzy logic today has an important impact not only in how it was applied at first (i.e., to computer technology) but also in how its impact extends to how we perceive the world and how we make sense of it.

Fuzzy logic changes our comfortable "logical" assumptions that have come down to us from the Aristotelian or classical way of reasoning. This approach helps us to deal with the uncertainty that grows out of the ever-evolving complexity inherent in our global society. Our old binary approach in which everything was black or white and true or false does not help us cope with the ever-increasing grays and middle ground societies and businesses are confronted with today. For today's business leaders this fuzzy logic approach provides a pragmatic and practical tool to help us cope with diversity and ever-growing complexity in doing business.

Business leaders and their organizations must understand that this present economic reality does not negate the current systemic organizational approach and analyses that epitomize our Western ways of doing business. It is not, and we must make certain it does not become, an either/or situation. Rather, we need a new way of imagining what is truly meaningful and profitable. We must go beyond seeking solutions to our economic problems, concerns, and ethical business conundrums in a series of yes or no dictums. We must not limit ourselves exclusively to rational/logical patterns, propositions, and laws and codes. Instead, we must imagine new perspectives with more universal value-laden choices. In this regard it is helpful to read Stephen Young's (executive director of the Caux Research Round Table) book *Moral Capitalism.* In it he imaginatively explores guidelines for a moral capitalism and advocates stewardship in business globally.

It's Not Business as Usual

Given the current global economic scenario with the multiple dimensions and webs of financial interactions, diversity, complexity, interdependence, and relatedness, who can be so naïve as to think that it will be business as usual? Can anyone possibly harbor the simplistic hope that all we need to do is "tweak" the system? Are there so-called business leaders who believe that all we need to do is complete some cultural diversity and sensitivity lessons to be successful on the global economic scene? Indeed, it certainly takes a great deal of fuzzy logic to grasp today's economic scene.

This is not to suggest that economic reality has changed; what has changed is the perception of economic reality. Business today must embrace an expanded notion of the essential creative role of imagination. Only with imagination can leaders foster and encourage greater flexibility, engage in more penetrating economic explorations, and conceive alternative future scenarios. The objective of this expanded role for imagination is not reinvention or reengineering; that is simply changing what already is. Neither is the purpose of expanding our imaginations to achieve incremental change, to do better what we are already doing. Imagination should and must be deployed to *transform* business and the ethics of doing business, to do what we have never done and never even thought of doing before. Admittedly, neither the task nor the goal is easily defined or clearly delineated. In fact, it's a bit fuzzy, isn't it? That's why it requires imagination.

In *The World Is Flat*, Thomas L. Friedman speaks directly to the essential component of imagination: "The most important attribute you can have is creative imagination—the ability to be the first on your block to figure out how all the enabling tools can be put together in new and exciting ways to create products, communities, opportunities, and profits. That has always been America's strength, because America was, and for now still is, the world's greatest dream machine."

THE MONDRAGON EXPERIMENT

As one example of this expansion of imagination, the Mondragon Experiment is a distinctively creative and innovative approach to doing good business while doing very good ethics. Currently successful and not very well known in the global business community, this free enterprise, business cooperative–type initiative operates in the Basque region of northern Spain, centered in the town of Mondragon.

The cooperative spirit has always been a characteristic of Basque culture. The region's long industrial tradition extends back to medieval times. Unfortunately, the Basque people found their region in ruins in the early 1940s, on the losing side of the Spanish Civil War. Then in 1941, General Franco's troops captured José María Arizmendiarrieta, a Roman Catholic priest who worked as a Basque Army journalist, and subjected him to a death-penalty court martial for rebellion. Luckily for Don José María, he was found not guilty on a technicality.

For the next fifteen years, Don José María initiated successful apprentice schools and technical training for the young people of the Basque region. In 1956, with the very young people he had trained, he founded the first manufacturing business cooperative, a new business enterprise that produced paraffin heaters and cookers. Don José María's vision was to form this profit-making enterprise while fostering his socially responsible ethical business values:

> Hand in hand, of one mind, renewed, united in work through work, in our small land we shall create a more human environment for everyone and we shall improve this land. We shall include villages and towns in our new equality; the people and everything else, ever forward. Nobody shall be slave or master of anyone, everyone shall simply work for the benefit of everyone else, and we shall have to behave differently in the way we work. This shall be our human and progressive union—a union which can be created by the people.

Expansion ensued; he established four other cooperatives. Success and profits flowed in, and so too the need for new capital to support these successes. So, like any creative and imaginative capitalist would do, Don José María launched his own cooperative bank, the Caja Laboral Popular, in 1959.

Over the next forty-five years, the hallmarks of Don José María's ventures continued to be more and more innovation, evergreater business success, and benefits to more and more people. They started new schools. They established forty-one other cooperatives. They created a research center for technological advancement. They opened new branches of their bank. And they founded the University of Mondragon. In 2004, the industrial and distribution sales of the Mondragon-based employee-owned cooperatives were 10.5 billion euros; the balance sheet revealed assets of 18.5 billion euros. The cooperatives employ 70,884 people. Their industrial sector recorded a 9.4 percent increase in sales. International sales increased by 9.6 percent, and the cooperatives developed nineteen new production plants, giving them forty-eight plants in fourteen different countries. They are now listed as one of the top five hundred companies in Europe. All this started as a result of the imagination of a local Basque priest back in 1941. (We have barely skimmed the surface of this fascinating and imaginative story. William and Kathleen Whyte's book, *Making Mondragon,* provides an excellent detailed account of the Mondragon cooperatives.)

Don José María's new, innovative business model—which thrives to this day—flows from basic principles that underpin the business ethic of the cooperatives, as well as from the imaginative dynamics that he imbued in his business plans. The core components of the Contract of Association, according to which every Mondragon cooperative is organized, adhere to the following basic principles.

Basic Principles

1. All those who work in a cooperative must be shareholders. No one can be a shareholder who does not work for the cooperative. In other words, the system is based on combining, indissolubly, the roles of workers and employer. This means that every worker, after a short trial period, is required to put up an initial capital stake. In exceptional circumstances the cooperative may hire other workers but their number may not exceed 5 percent of the total membership. Usually such cases concern persons with special skills or knowledge whose services are required for a limited period.

2. All the cooperatives recognize the principle of solidarity in two ways. The first way can be described as internal; it affects wage and salary differentials. The maximum range of salary differentials is set at one to three. That means that there are no people earning gross wages greater than three times the lowest paid member of the cooperative. In exceptional circumstances the

differential may be as great as 1:4.5 for extra hours worked, continued absence from home on cooperative business, etc. There is also a second, external rule: average wages are fixed annually at the level paid for similar jobs in comparable capitalist enterprises within the region.

3. The Open Door Principle means that membership in the cooperative shall not be restricted but open to all whose services are appropriate. A member joins voluntarily and agrees to abide by the rules and accept the responsibilities membership entails.

4. The Democratic Principle, as its name implies, declares that all authority is ultimately conferred by the democratic votes of all the members of a cooperative. Those who are ultimately responsible for administering the cooperative are elected and are accountable to the membership.

Organization

1. *General Assembly* Following the basic rule of one worker, one vote, the General Assembly is the expression of the membership, and meets at least once yearly in ordinary session and can be called when necessary for an extraordinary meeting. It is empowered in an ordinary session to examine and approve the accounts and balance sheet of the previous financial year.

   It is also empowered to deal with matters concerning initial capital contributions of new members; a requirement for further capital contributions or rights issues; the approval of internal rules; and the establishment and modification of organizational norms for administering and carrying out the different services within the cooperative.

2. *The Board of Directors* The General Assembly elects the members of the board of directors, to which it delegates the power to decide policy. Board members, always between three and

twelve in number, are elected for four years, with half being replaceable every two years.

They meet at least once a month, and decisions are made by democratic vote of those present at the meeting, with the chairman casting a vote in the case of a tie.

3. *Account Control Board* This board is comprised of three members, directly elected by the General Assembly for a term of four years. Their basic function is to control and inspect the accounts and documents of each cooperative to determine if the established accounts have been followed.

4. *The Management* Comprised of one person, generally, management has the executive function of running the cooperative as a productive unit. Appointed by the board of directors for a term of four years, the management is responsible and accountable to the board and, through the board, ultimately to the cooperative's membership gathered in the General Assembly.

5. *The Management Council* This council is an advisory and consultative body, formed by managers and high executives of the company. Meetings must take place at least once a month.

6. *The Social Council* This council, original to Mondragon cooperatives, is the elected voice of the members of the cooperative with wide prescriptive and advisory powers in all aspects of personnel management. Its decisions are binding in such matters as accident prevention, safety and hygiene at work, social security, wage levels, administration of social funds, and so forth.

To elect the Social Council, the members vote by department, one representative from each. The Social Council generally meets once a month.

As well as being an advisory body, the Social Council transmits the information from the board of directors to the workers and the workers' opinions to the board of directors.

Predictably, this successful and expansive business model has many more refinements and dynamics that do not lend themselves to further elaboration here. This particular enterprise was singled out not necessarily for others to emulate, but rather as a striking example of what imagination can bring to future successful business enterprises that are grounded in ethical business dynamics.

While Cargill is not a cooperative, it is increasingly a privately owned, global enterprise focused on generating profit through satisfying human needs in the areas of nutrition, agriculture and food, and, recently, energy.

Cargill, along with numerous farmer-owned cooperatives and other entrepreneurs, is building alcohol refineries that produce ethanol from corn or biodiesel from edible oils such as soybean oil. They are driven by imagination, profit, and national interest. Ethanol, along with appropriate increases in U.S. fuel efficiency standards, could help wean this country from its unhealthy dependence on imported oil. Already, Cargill scientists are working on next-generation fuel crops, producing ethanol from agricultural and forest wastes, a process measurably more difficult than extraction from the corn kernel. When Cargill scientists achieve this breakthrough in the future, increased quantities of alternative fuel could be available.

Some in both government and industry continue to debate whether the world is running out of oil. At the same time, people with foresight are trying to counter the impact of profligate U.S. demand for oil, compounded by burgeoning demand for oil from countries such as China and India, factors that have doubled the price of gasoline at the pump over the last four years. Employing renewable and waste products to create alcohol fuels takes imagination and courage. There is also a challenge in this—alternative fuels are using increasing amounts of crops that have traditionally been used solely for food.

WHAT THE EXECS ARE SAYING

Bob Kierlin is a far cry from the dazzling, dynamic Baby Suggs of Toni Morrison's *Beloved*. Kierlin is an unassuming, understated capitalist who has bettered lives and created hundreds of millions in wealth for himself, employees, and other shareholders.

Kierlin, a smug critic might say, is a successful small-town guy with a surprising wit. We know him as engineer who sought his own enterprise, an MBA who spent his first two years in Venezuela serving others in the Peace Corps. Plus, he is one of America's least affected, most egoless executives.

Kierlin and four of his friends invested $31,000 apiece and a lot of sweat into a fledgling company in 1967 that they called Fastenal. The company they started today employs more than eight thousand around the globe. They imagined a better company, a better product, and a better place to work. They focused on ethical capitalism and how it could be perpetuated around the world. "Capitalism must raise the living standards for the people on the low end, not just the upper echelon," said the chairman and founder of the Minnesota-based manufacturer and retailer of nuts, bolts, and all kinds of industrial fasteners. "It's up to the leaders of the company to do that."

Kierlin never took a salary from the company he founded of more than $130,000—a pittance by U.S. CEO standards. He's been recognized as an exceptionally low-paid boss by the *Wall Street Journal*, as well as a lot of happy shareholders.

Conversely, in China and wherever else Fastenal operates, the company finds it is a benefit to pay the highest wages and offer the best benefits. By hiring and retaining good employees, Fastenal has developed imagination, work ethic, and productivity that have made it a top performer in its industry.

Kierlin built tens of millions in wealth for himself through the value of Fastenal's stock. He and his employees, many of whom have built six- and seven-figure fortunes in the stock of the company over the years, may be America's best example of how ethical business can lead to expansion, prosperity, and fortunes for imaginative owners, employees, and their communities.

In 1987, Fastenal went public in an initial public offering that gave the company a market value of $30 million. Kierlin, since-retired and currently chairman, and the other directors of the company wanted to raise expansion capital, allow employees to become owners of a company with liquidity, and make it easier for the original owners to start donating some of their wealth in the company to charitable and educational institutions.

And how! Today Fastenal, which has posted solid long-term performance, has grown from a regional company to a global supplier with a shareholder value of $5.7 billion.

"I have an abundant belief that the capitalist system gives us the opportunity to do good things as a result of the economic well-being it can create," Kierlin said. "But if you have poor leadership, if you don't share the benefits, the results will be bad. Everybody in the organization has to be in on it."

To that end, Kierlin, a modest-living millionaire residing in the river town of Winona, Minnesota, takes pride in Fastenal employees who have good jobs or comfortable retirements and who can afford to educate their children. He has also directly contributed millions of dollars of his stock-market gains in the form of scholarship and other funds for Winona-area students at three secondary and post-secondary schools and other educational institutions.

And if that's not enough, Kierlin has created and financed other companies, such as Hiawatha Broadband, the cable TV and Internet service provider in southeastern Minnesota. He then turned over 40 percent of the ownership to area educational institutions. The better the cable company does in the Winona area, the more opportunity and investment for local students.

Now, that's imagination—even Baby Suggs might agree!

CONCLUSION

For any of us, but especially for business leaders constantly held to account for the next quarter's profits, it is understandably difficult to waver from current conventional wisdom and so-called best practices. Yet, at some level of our dialogue and our consciousness, we are aware that there is a qualitatively different global business platform being constructed right before our eyes. No one yet has the final picture of how that will look since no one is the single architect responsible for the finished product. Quite assuredly, there will be a prominent place on that new global economic platform for socially responsible structures, if there is to be any market at all remaining in a world where terror and intolerance are rampant.

No one has described today's urgent need for a new imagination better than Maxine Greene, a committed and dedicated educator, who wrote, "To break with ordinariness and stock response is, at any age, to achieve a new readiness, a new ripeness. Not only will there be awareness of things in their particularity of beauty and variety and form. There will be a fresh orientation to the search for meaning in the many spheres of life . . .

"People may be brought to watch and to listen with unceasing wide-awakeness, attentiveness, and care. And they may be brought to discover multiple ways to look at blackbirds and whales and riverbanks and city streets, looking at things as if they might be otherwise than they are" ("Aesthetic Literacy in General Education," *Philosophy and Education*, 80th Yearbook of the National Society for the Study of Education (1981)).

With these imaginative words, we are inspired to add another ingredient into our modern-day elaboration of business ethics:

Business ethics requires business leaders to have the courage to use their imaginations to find new and innovative ways to place profiting people in the equation for business profits.

Take Action Questions

1. How can we evaluate and assess the business environment in another country with fairness and objectivity?

2. How can business leaders enhance organizational receptiveness to new and innovative ways that may make business better and more profitable for shareholders, employees, and customers in the long run, but not necessarily in the short term?

3. What is the role of consultants in promoting innovation and creativity in organizations? Do they help or hinder the process?

4. What can business leaders do to become innovative and imaginative leaders?

5. What steps can be taken by employees to become more innovative and imaginative workers?

CHAPTER 6

Keep Religion Out of Business Ethics if You Believe God Is on Your Side

T HERE IS A STORY TOLD about two very different monks living in a monastery: one, a seasoned, aging, serene, holy monk; and the other, shall we say, a bit worldly. We'll call the holy one Brother Serene, and the other monk Brother Hip. One day, Brother Hip told Brother Serene of his nighttime dream that an angel came to him and said "Brother Hip, the Lord sent me to let you know that He is giving you a choice to receive His gift to you of either all knowledge and holiness, or of all the money you desire—*but* you must choose only one." Brother Serene excitedly asked Brother Hip, "Well, which did you choose?" (Even though, if the truth be told, Brother Serene was fairly certain that Brother Hip had chosen the money.) Brother Hip said sadly, "Well, I didn't choose either, because just as I was about tell the angel my choice, I awoke and the angel disappeared." "Don't despair, Brother Hip," said Brother Serene. "Tonight if the angel appears again, immediately give him your choice so that he doesn't depart from you too soon." The next morning Brother Hip ran over to holy Brother Serene and gasped, "Brother Serene, I did as you suggested; I gave my choice immediately to the angel, and my choice was instantly granted to me. Thank you for your wonderful advice." Intrigued, yet certain he knew the answer, Brother Serene perfunctorily queried, "And, tell me, good Brother Hip, which did you choose? All the knowledge and holiness or the money?" Brother Hip responded, "I took all the knowledge and holiness, of course!" A long pause ensued while the holy monk decided how he should respond without displaying his significant skepticism about what Brother Hip just told him. So Brother Serene politely asked, "Brother Hip, could you say something to me now that may help me appreciate that you, indeed, have this great knowledge and holiness?" Brother Hip spent a brief moment thinking about a response to Brother Serene that would make him believe that he now had the gift of all knowledge and holiness. He answered, "I should have taken the money!"

Perhaps Brother Hip truly did receive that very special gift of knowledge and holiness. His unexpected choice sheds light both on an important problem religions cause in today's world and on how that problem affects economic global dynamics. It is not our intention to put forth an indictment of religion, per se. Rather, we seek to mount an assault on the distortions of religion occasioned by the growing and persistent presence of ideologues who attempt to "defend" their ideologies under the guise of explaining their religion. How can we possibly expect global economic stability or progress, if at the root of global terrorism are religious ideologues believing God is on their side? How can we hold out any hope for business ethics to be developed and accepted when the various religions around the world cannot coexist peacefully? Let us explore further how this sensitive and complicated interrelation between religions and economics plays out today.

A PERVERSION OF REASON

Whether the topic is human life, economic life, culture, education, or religion, we should understand ideology as a systematic body of concepts, integrated assertions, and theories that constitute a view of reality. For intellectuals, ideology has held a powerful and influential appeal that can be traced back to the efforts of the aforementioned French Enlightenment, which produced a set of "mechanical laws" to explain human nature. Today's ideologues, irrespective of country, culture, or religion, share with the proponents of the Enlightenment this mechanistic, rigid style of thinking. Kenneth Minogue, in his book *Alien Powers: The Pure Theory of Ideology*, warns of the ideologue's tendency to consistently lean toward certainty (i.e., "my" certainty). Minogue convincingly places ideology in the perspective of a perversion of reason. In essence, ideology is to reason as gluttony is to fine dining! The grave danger inherent in any ideology, some say, is its propensity to become an intellectual chameleon, since it appears sometimes as a science, other times as a philosophy, or oftentimes and most dangerously as a religion. Religious ideology becomes an insidious enemy to economic global development since it casts a shadow over the human imagination by offering neat ideological formulae under the guise of "total truth."

Keep in mind that religion is not the problem; the problem is religious ideologies that prostitute the wholesome and good principles and values of world religions. Throughout history, religious ideologies have cast dark—and, in some cases, evil—shadows over our globe. By attesting to the so-called principles that emanate from their ideologies rather than from the basic truths of their religion, religious ideologues—even to this day—justify detestable acts of human travesty and terror. Relying on their perversion of reason, they seek to justify the ethics of their actions.

Keeping religion out of business ethics is not meant to diminish the importance of a spiritual message. Instead, it should encourage business leaders to develop new outlets, to explore new discoveries, and to take new risks that involve the integration of their religious faith with their business. The most meaningful and critical risk will involve the creation and implementation of a new language, a new way of talking about business, about profits, and about people.

Ideologues of every persuasion contribute to this intellectual prostitution of principles and values. We live in an era in which indignation has become a way of life. Some conservatives are disposed to proclaim that everybody should "pay their own way." Some liberals ceaselessly promote a Robin Hood–esque economic system. Some academicians elevate political correctness to the highest priority. And some religions place all their hopes in the occurrence of some miraculous epiphany. Today, ideologues of all types abound and insist that adherence to their principles and beliefs offers the only opportunity for emerging from the shadows of destruction; instead, their fervor and their frenzy bind us tighter with the shackles of distrust and terror that inevitably generate economic instability.

Distrust, Hatred, and Instability

Even a superficial overview of current events highlights a strange phenomenon in the socio-religious realm. We can readily and easily observe both the expanding worldwide skepticism about organized religions (ideologue skeptics) and the concurrent growing worldwide movement toward religious fundamentalism (ideologue fundamentalists). Ideologue skeptics breed suspicion, distrust, and paranoia about organized religions, claiming that the core values of peace and human dignity promoted by established religions are to be despised and discarded as nothing more than futile plots that infringe on people's individual and personal freedoms. Rigid ideologue fundamentalists take their suspicion, distrust, and paranoia to more outrageous (not higher, just more outrageous) levels, as they replace the core values of peace and human dignity of their own religions with cacophonous and rabid calls to strike down the infidels, kill the unbelievers, and terrorize everyone into submission to their vision of "God's will be done." Both the skeptics and the fundamentalists lead us to pose the question: How can the dynamics of global economics be functional when ideologues, in the name of religion, take on the armor of secular power and increasingly resort to hostility and terror? In a world shaped by these religious ideologues, just doing business carries with it unprecedented challenges; doing business ethics may be beyond the scope of possibility.

The ideological rifts in our world, rifts that are growing in both scope and intensity, constitute a monumental challenge to those who seek universally acceptable business principles and actions. Philip Jenkins, professor of history and religious studies at Pennsylvania State University, in his book, *The Next Christendom: The Coming of Global Christianity*, concludes that by the year 2050, sub-Saharan Africa will have surpassed Europe as the leading global center of Christianity. At that same midcentury point, the populations of Brazil, Mexico, the Philippines, Nigeria, Congo, and the United States of America will include more than 600 million Christians. The significance of these projections is found not in the aggregate raw numbers, but one level lower, in the details. It is Pentecostals that constitute the greatest wave of future Christian growth. And, Pentecostalism, born in the early twentieth century, emphasizes the power of personal faith, biblical literalism, and apocalyptic visions—not exactly a contributing and soothing force for religious global peaceful coexistence!

Bernard Lewis, respected scholar and author, broadens our understanding of the potent dangers inherent in the advancement of these fundamentalist ideologies in his recent book about the contemporary Muslim world, *The Crisis of Islam—Holy War and Unholy Terror*. Basing his conclusions on research into historiography, jurisprudence, and culture in Islamic society in the Middle East, Lewis identifies what is being put forth as Islam's theological basis for jihad and martyrdom. Regardless of one's political viewpoint, a reading of Lewis's research will lead to the inescapable conclusion that neither terrorism nor the mandate to fight the infidels has a convincing or supportable basis in Islamic scripture. Terrorism runs counter to centuries of Islamic religion and tradition; but not for the Muslim ideologue! The picture that emerges from reviewing both Lewis's study of contemporary Muslim jihad-focused radicalism and Jenkins's research highlighting the new tidal wave of Christian fundamentalists (problematic, but certainly less warlike than Middle Eastern ideologues) is that of a wall of turbulent water crashing and smashing over any semblance of political, religious, or economic order.

The simultaneous confluence of these movements is worthy of our attention. Jenkins predicts that by 2050 approximately twenty of the twenty-five largest nations will be predominantly or entirely Christian or Muslim, with at least ten of these nations being sites of intense conflict. Jenkins predicts that these near-future conflicts will make the bloody religious wars of the sixteenth century look like calisthenics. Ours is a shrinking global society in which the cultural and ideological forces of the extreme fringes of world religions—not their true spiritual faith—quantitatively and qualitatively shake apart our world economic equilibrium. Under these circumstances, how can we hold out any hope that we can look to religions to help us unfold and develop ethical business actions in a global economy?

Simply stated, in our world today the great religions play a radically different role than most of us would like to believe. It is today's global tragedy that the ideologues within religions—rather than being part of the solution to our global conflicts—have been significant, contributing, and causal factors to the problems we face. The insidious perspectives promulgated by religious fundamentalist ideologues around the globe alienate peoples, nations, religions, cultures, and economies because they perpetuate environments of distrust, hatred, and instability.

The dynamics generated by these religious ideologues lead us to a critical conclusion, one that we offer both with forceful conviction and with sensitivity, because we are quite aware of its propensity to be misunderstood: keep religion out of business ethics, if you believe God is on your side! This is not to suggest that the faith-filled and spiritual truths of all world religions today are the problem. Emphatically no! We assert that the problem lies in permitting those truly spiritual thoughts to be mediated to the world by the religious ideologues. When that occurs, the incontrovertible evidence supports our contention: keep religion out of business ethics, if you believe God is on your side!

A New Language Is Needed

Given the precarious circumstances occasioned by the global threat of religious fundamentalist ideologues, business leaders must find ways to create a new language that will allow true faith-filled religious people—with all their richness and diversity—to comprehend the most common, agreed upon, universalizable values that place the dignity of people front and center.

This new language involves business leaders talking to people with words and ideas that are attractive to them and that they understand. It means finding new ways to explain why treating people with fairness and with the dignity they deserve as "workers" in business is not based only on sectarian religious beliefs, but rather is part of doing good business (i.e., business profits when people profit).

One may legitimately ask, "Why do you believe that the duty to create a new language falls on business leaders instead of church leaders?" The answer is apparent: church leaders have no track record of success in the endeavor of creating that language. Though well-intentioned, these religious leaders are hamstrung by their doctrines, rubrics, rules, and customs, and by the internal ideologues, who won't permit them to embrace others whose approach to and explanations of the truth may differ from their own.

We believe that the business leader occupies a uniquely privileged position in this global quagmire, for it is the business leader who can be a spiritual catalyst by engaging in and promoting innovative and ethical business dynamics to promote his or her business and stakeholder interests. The business leader can use his or her unique position to imagine, create, and effect both a model and a nomenclature for ethical business that can achieve universal acceptance and will thrive to the extent that the resulting commerce benefits workers, their families, customers, and communities.

The contention by ersatz religious believers that "God is on my side" functions as the fuse for many of the global and economic problems we have discussed earlier. True religious believers—in all religions—know that God is on the side of everyone who is committed to doing good; by contrast, religious ideologues focus solely on being good. Today's citizens and business leaders on our shrinking globe have a golden opportunity to forge a new alliance between the sacred and the secular worlds, if only we find the courage and the intelligence to discard our pretensions and our rigid propensity to see the sacred and the secular as opposites, as competitors, and as mutually exclusive. The floodlight of history illumines countless examples of the unspeakable horrors and destructive tendencies of both worlds, especially when they are not tempered by consideration of the other.

After all, the state charters American business to operate first and foremost in the "public interest." When Jesus Christ banished the money changers from the temple, the fundamental message was that commerce that benefits only the financiers is a sin. When

Enron executives set up sham partnerships to benefit a few individuals and book phony profits it violated law and morality.

The Bible could be debated indefinitely—and often is by the so-called fundamentalists—on matters of homosexuality, the role of women, and why environmental stewardship doesn't matter since the end of the world is almost at hand anyway. But great theologians of many Christian faiths find repeatedly in the New Testament the spoken words of Jesus Christ exhorting us about a special obligation that the powerful have for the children, the poor, and the dispossessed. Scripture also quotes Jesus frequently telling stories and giving examples of a second chance for sinners and the power of forgiveness. And in the parables we find His words about the marvel and power of the natural environment and its connection to the spiritual world.

Spiritual business leaders are those who generate new and better products that benefit people at reasonable cost, seek reasonable profits, and practice stewardship of employees and the environment. In addition, business leaders who aspire to be spiritual reward labor fairly, quite often with some appropriate level of shared ownership.

It is written that we are only temporary stewards of wealth and this world. Ultimately, we must pass on all that we have and all that we have enjoyed in better shape to the next generation. That is the privilege and obligation of stewardship.

The tenets of both Christianity and Islam speak with conviction to the dignity of the worker, to the rights of each of us as equals before God, to education, health, and opportunity. Both faith traditions also call for the owners of capital to be more than just money changers, to be insightful and compassionate investors.

Despite the protestations of some, business is not the enemy of religion! Indeed, business—while realizing unprecedented success, generating meaningful profit levels, and serving as the catalyst for unfathomable innovation—may become the facilitator of religious and spiritual truth in this third millennium, as paradoxical as that may at first seem.

WHAT THE EXECS ARE SAYING

Brother Michael O'Hern, the veteran chief executive officer of Christian Brothers Investment Services, Inc. (CBIS), and his organization are helping corporate America to do ethics better through the confluence of "faith and finance." CBIS is an investment advisory company registered under the Investment Advisory Act. Brother O'Hern oversees $4 billion in pension and other assets that CBIS manages for many Catholic organizations. CBIS encourages companies whose stock they own to do ethics better by acting as responsible shareholders in the long-term interest of all constituents.

CBIS has provided competitive returns compared with its performance benchmarks and competitors by aligning investments with its socially responsible mission, which also has changed the behavior of some companies. "When we look at corporations, we look at human enterprises and we want to see our values as owners reflected," said Brother O'Hern, a seventeen-year investment-industry veteran. "By and large, most people in companies want to do good."

CBIS, which was founded by Brother Louis DeThomasis in 1982, believes that the missions of financial and social return are inseparable. And CBIS, as a steward of its investors' money, engages in dialogue with companies as needed.

In short, it's no good to be an owner of an industrial company that pollutes the air, doesn't replace the trees it harvests, or fouls the water in furtherance of short-term profit. That's bad business and bad ethics: without clean air, more trees, and clean water there is no long-term future for business—or humanity.

Here are a few specific examples of the work of CBIS as a corporate owner:

- In response to a surprisingly strong shareholder vote in 2003 and further dialogue with CBIS and other shareholder groups, American Electric Power, the nation's largest coal-burning utility, agreed in 2004 to report to shareholders on the financial risks it faces from the high level of greenhouse gases, mercury, and other toxic emissions produced by its coal-fired plants, which are known to pollute air and water and threaten health. Since this model agreement was struck, a number of other utilities have decided to produce similar reports and many are working to cap and reduce emissions through environmental controls or more efficient systems that actually produce more energy and less pollution.

- CBIS and its clients have long been concerned with human rights abuses in the African and other foreign operations of mining and oil companies. In 2004, after a year of dialogue, Occidental Petroleum agreed to develop a human rights policy that will include independent monitoring and local community involvement for its operation in the developing world. Similarly, CBIS is working with Sears Roebuck and Alcoa to develop a human rights code of conduct to govern the treatment and financial consideration of workers who labor for their suppliers in developing countries.

- Tyco, once one of America's biggest industrial polluters through several subsidiaries, agreed to perform an environmental impact analysis and report the results in an effort to monitor the effects of its toxic emissions.

Other major corporations have opted to adopt this trend toward environmental responsibility. In 2005 the CEO of General Electric, Jeff Immelt, pledged that the world's largest industrial company would cut its pollution as it produces more products and focus on the highest levels of energy conservation and sustainable development.

Immelt said the United States has fallen behind European competitors in this regard. He gave the speech in Washington D.C., in what was viewed as something of a slap at a U.S. administration that has failed to set energy conservation, alternative energy, and pollution control as a national imperative—even as demand for oil and gasoline prices soar.

The chairmen of British Petroleum and Ford Motor Company have created market-driven visions for their companies, influenced by shareholder concerns, that are built on less oil and pollution and more efficiency, renewable fuels, and technology that can be produced around the globe—not just dependency on oil-laden, corrupt regimes that control increasingly scarce oil and natural gas.

Moreover, concerned shareholders like CBIS in the United States and elsewhere want operations in Asia and Africa to be market leaders and pacesetters in the areas of environment and human rights, including fair treatment for workers.

Capitalists such as Bob Kierlin of Fastenal and Warren Staley of Cargill, for example, pay their Chinese workforces market competitive wages and expect the plant conditions to meet environmental and health standards. Their companies are stressing education of workers and advancement of families. This is how worker-oriented capitalism can benefit the world's poor.

"We're concerned with the standards and the principles," Brother O'Hern said. "It's not necessarily that we're after the same pay as in the United States. But we don't just want these companies to seek the lowest common denominator (in wages and working conditions). The ill effects can fall disproportionately on the poor."

It is good business to pay workers sufficiently and treat workers well so that they can afford to feed, house, and educate their families—and wear the Nike tennis shoes that they work so hard to make.

CONCLUSION

Remember the insight from the story of Brother Hip and Brother Serene at the outset of this chapter: "I should have taken the money!" Indeed, Brother Hip understood the emerging new language of the third millennium, a language that rejects the notion that the worlds of the sacred and the secular are antagonistic to each other. The inability of many to speak or understand the new language has produced an artificial fragmentation or split that has led to rampant ineffectiveness in the worlds of both religion and business.

In the foreword to a monograph written by Brother Louis DeThomasis, entitled *Social Justice—A Christian Pragmatic Response In Today's World*, the Rev. Paschal Phillips, O.C.S.O., a monk from the Trappist Abbey of Our Lady of Guadalupe in Lafayette, Oregon, provides an insightful comment about this artificial split between a higher (or spiritual) and lower (or worldly) understanding:

> Interestingly enough, both Jesus himself and Saint Paul seemed to be quite free from this fragmentation which affects modern man ... When Jesus wanted to make a point he habitually reached for an analogy from the economic world around him. This tendency of mind is slightly hidden from us because the economic entrepreneurs of his day went around disguised as shepherds, fishermen, sowers of seeds. Time has wrapped them in a certain poetic mist so that a modern parable about auto mechanics or tractor drivers sounds subtly irreverent.
>
> Paul seems to have felt even more at home with commercial analogies to spiritual truths. He dares to describe the whole inner secret of salvation in terms of the commercial practice of his day, whereby notes of indebtedness were torn in half upon repayment. Words from the marketplace such as *redemption* were used by Paul with such emphasis that they have by now assumed an almost totally religious meaning. We have quite forgotten they started out as a metaphor!

We assert unequivocally that relying on economics alone or religion alone cannot and will not lead to viable, sustainable business ethics in a global economic environment replete with competing values, customs, and cultures, especially if that environment also allows combative religious ideologues to flourish. Contemporary global economic reality—defined in part by the concomitant compression of distance, communication, and finance through technology and the inevitable continuing evolution in those areas—requires us to discover and employ a new way to talk about this so that we can be understood. A triad of global spheres—the political, the economic, and the religious/cultural—has given birth to a new inextricable and complex symbiotic relationship never known before to humanity, to business, or to religions.

Thus, we include another ingredient into our mix to understand business ethics for the future:

Business ethics must recognize that it is not business as usual. Faith and finance can no longer be separated in the future. Business leaders must find a new language that will be understood in this increasingly fragmented world.

Take Action Questions

1. Is it possible to be an ethical businessperson without any religious beliefs? Would organizations operate more efficiently if all employees were of the same religious faith?

2. Is the Christian admonition "to render unto Caesar that which is Caesar's and unto God that which is God's" a clear mandate that supports the fact that religion has no place in business?

Take Action Questions, continued

3. Is it true that the Christian admonition "we will always have the poor with us" is a clear mandate that social justice is really not a Christian value to be brought into the business realm?

4. Is it possible to act ethically and fairly within an organization without knowing the religions (or lack thereof) of the people within the organization?

CHAPTER 7

It Takes Faith

W E BEGAN THIS BOOK ASKING the meaning of the term *business ethics*. If we were to pursue an answer to that question only by surveying the volumes in the ivory towers of the academic world (a task that would consume a couple of decades), we would undoubtedly find frustration with the intellectual sophistications and gyrations that flourish in that type of literature. While the intricacies and nuances of much of the academic discourse provide limited value to the professional businessperson seeking practical guidance, continued research and writing on ethics and related topics must be supported and encouraged as they are essential components for those looking for a deeper understanding of ethical business actions in the real world. But the true value to the professional businessperson occurs only after these academic treatises are distilled and then translated into the pragmatic everyday world of business dynamics.

Unfortunately, in too many instances the distillation seemingly runs amok and we are left with popularized books and articles that are nothing more than simplistic, pietistic, gratuitous expositions of the "business ethics made easy" genre. Reality, along with basic common sense, tells us that neither sleep-inducing academic tomes nor *CliffsNotes* approaches contribute meaningfully to either an understanding or a transformation of business ethics.

Thus, the foundational premises that we have interwoven throughout this book are as follows:

- Business ethics is not simply an academic subject matter.
- Business ethics is not just a "soft" exercise, such as "Would your mother be embarrassed if she knew what you were doing?"
- Business ethics is not confined to just religious and spiritual dimensions.
- Business ethics is not just a codification of dos and don'ts.
- Business ethics is not just a simplistic golden rule.
- Business ethics is not some overly complex, impossible dynamic.
- Business ethics *is* all of the above and more: Sometimes business ethics is science. Most times business ethics is an art. *Always*, business ethics is action!

Therefore, it is easy to make the connection that fundamentally business ethics is a faith-filled dynamic of practical and profitable business decisions and actions. This is not to say that business ethics is religion based. Perhaps the following story will help clarify how faith, but not religion, is a significant part of business ethics.

An extremely poor inner-city parish invited a college theology professor to be the featured speaker at its monthly evening religious education program. Parishioners informed him that due to their lack of resources, they could not offer him a stipend. But they did invite him and a guest of his choosing to be their guests at the parish potluck dinner that preceded the program. The professor thought it would be a good learning experience for his ten-year-old son to join him that evening; perhaps, he thought, his son would recognize the privileged life that he lived.

When father and son arrived at this poor inner-city church for the potluck dinner, they found all the parishioners, though poor, dressed in their Sunday best for the occasion. The professor turned to his son and said, "Son, look at all these poor people and see how nicely they are dressed. What can you learn from this?" The boy looked confused and shrugged his shoulders and muttered, "Gee, I don't know, Daddy." "Well, son," the father replied, "even though these are poor people who can't afford all the expensive clothes that you have, they are neat and clean, and they look nice without designer jeans and the latest fashions. Do you see that? Have you learned something new now?" "Yes, Daddy," said the son.

Father and son then joined all the parishioners in the parish hall for a magnificent dinner with plenty of healthy and delicious food. At the end of the meal the father turned to his son once again and said, "What can you learn from this, son?" Again the little boy shrugged his shoulders and said, "Gee, I don't know." "Well," the father replied, "even though these poor people can't afford expensive food like we have at home, they have prepared a wonderful, tasty meal for us from simple and inexpensive food items because they all worked together and shared with one another. Do you see that? Have you learned something new now?" "Yes," said the son.

Then the entire congregation went into the church and listened attentively as the professor gave his talk. They applauded and publicly thanked him very much, and said, once again, that they were sorry that they were unable to give him a stipend. When it was time to leave, a few members of the congregation began to escort father and son out of the church. As they walked the father bent over and whispered in his son's ear, "Son, when we get to the front door of the church, turn around to the altar and ask about the stained glass windows there. I want you to do that so I can secretly put a $100 bill into the offering box without the parishioners seeing me. Even though they are poor, son, they are very proud and they would never accept the gift." When they arrived at the front door, the son dutifully did as his father had said, and the father was able to slip the $100 bill into the offering box without anyone seeing him.

Minutes later, all the poor parishioners stood in front of the church to say goodbye to the professor and his son. Just as they reached their car parked in front of the church, they heard a group of parishioners running toward them, shouting for them to wait before driving off. One of the parishioners went over to the father, placed in his hand a $100 bill, and said, "We are so very happy and most pleasantly surprised that we are now able to give you a stipend of $100. As we were leaving church, we looked into the offering box and unknown to us some generous person had given us $100. Thank you so much, professor, for sharing your wisdom with us this evening." Though he tried to decline their generosity, they would not hear of it.

As they drove off the father turned to his son and said, "Did you learn from this, son?" This time, much to his surprise, the little boy said, "Oh yes, Daddy, I did learn something." Startled, the father asked his son what he learned. The little boy answered, "I learned that if you gave more, you would have gotten back more!"

An Unwavering Belief

Business ethics requires an unwavering belief, a faith, that doing good is good: good for you, good for others, good for business. Business ethics is not neat, clean, easily quantifiable, and a fast and sure track to specific calculable results. Like all matters of faith, it rests on a willingness and ability to accept that which cannot be verified empirically. Fundamentally, business ethics requires us to believe that whatever our endeavors, if we give more, we will indeed get back more.

While the faith we talk about here is not necessarily religious or philosophical, it is quite real and extraordinarily powerful. Like all faith, it fills the void that exists when empirical science or purely calculable reason alone cannot give full evidence of the phenomenon. To date, no philosopher or philosophy, no religious leader or religion, no moralist or moral code, indeed, no group or individual independently has provided us with a prima facie case for doing ethics in business. Yet each of these movements and each of these types of individuals contribute to and are essential forces in unfolding the mystery of why ethics makes sense for our world and for our global economy. By its very nature as a mystery, we know from the outset it will never be solved. A problem, on the other hand, has a solution; even though we may not have the solution right now, we know eventually we can solve the problem. A true mystery means that we know there is *no* solution that we will be able to discover. Instead, the mystery must be lived by embracing the spirit of the dynamic and energy that unfolds as we act upon our faith.

To this very point, William A. Schreyer, the then (1988) chairman and chief executive officer of Merrill Lynch & Co., Inc., wrote the preface to a monograph authored by Brother Louis DeThomasis entitled *Monasteries on Wall Street?* (The monograph was presented at the National Symposium on Socially Responsible Investing sponsored by Christian Brothers Investment Services, Inc., October 7, 1987, in San Francisco.) Schreyer observed the following.

> As the world of business, and consequently, the politics of the world, make all economic and political systems increasingly interdependent, American business leaders occupy a unique position. Able to penetrate the national boundaries that constrain politicians, their influence—and (that of) the billions of dollars in capital American firms can move at the press of a button—is worldwide.

The Wall Street I know is made up of thousands of people who are acutely aware of their responsibility to ethically invest the hard-earned savings of millions of Americans in ways that earn the greatest possible return. For those Wall Streeters, trust—not greed—is the coin of the realm.

Like the overwhelming majority of Americans, Wall Streeters do not believe that greed is a virtue. The do not believe that illegal or unethical behavior should go unpunished. They do not believe that life without a moral compass is a life worth living.

In fact, because their personal and professional reputations are based on a bedrock of trust and honesty, Wall Streeters rejoice when those few among us who break the rules of legal and ethical conduct are caught and punished to the fullest extent of the law.

The belief that acting ethically in business is a win-win-win situation requires an act of faith. The individual business leader wins. Free enterprise wins. The people win. If we give more, we will all get more—believe it! What we used to regard as a big world has shrunk markedly and the result is an evolving new global intimacy that has replaced classical industrial dynamics with large-scale interrelated economies and technologies. Transforming the complex equation of the impact of nations, economics, and people with conflicting values and nonaligned cultural persuasions into a formula for peaceful and profitable coexistence goes well beyond the capacity of the most sophisticated computer matrix. It requires something infinitely more advanced and at the same time so simple that it has existed since the creation of humankind: faith! The power of faith can transcend the sovereignty of nations, cultures, religions, and economies. This faith does not require the acquisition of an expansive and expensive new base of knowledge. All that is needed is a transformed imagination that will show us the wisdom that as we give more, we will get back more. In her book, *Moral Principles and Social Values*, Jennifer Trusted keenly observed, "It is the wise who know that to act morally is to fulfill the aspirations of human nature; this knowledge is, indeed, what makes them wise."

PROFIT—NOT A NECESSARY EVIL

It is in this context of an increasingly complex, shrinking global community that we find ourselves at the beginning of the third millennium. The practice of business ethics necessarily requires and embraces a deeply personal dimension, yet a personal dimension within a global societal milieu of humanistic, religious, economic, and ethical pluralism. In the vast spectrum of human and corporate decisions, business leaders must have a faith that is concurrently personal and universalizable so that they can be both leaders and risk-takers. Ideally, the business leader's faith springs from roots within the wonderful faith-filled values of the world's great religions. But even then the business leader's faith needs translation into a faith that is neither sectarian nor doctrinal. The central tenet of such a faith may be the belief that if I give more, I will get back more. Without question, the profit motive is a constitutive element in business. We believe that the profit motive should be neither rationalized away, nor considered a necessary evil. Why should we criticize or feel any guilt over businesses that strive to generate the rewards of profits? Do not all religions promise rewards of some type, material or spiritual, to their faith-filled adherents?

You have heard the saying that theologians study theology so that they can avoid hell and holy people study theology because they've been there. For both people of faith and atheists, the problem of evil has been ever present in the equation of living life. Even Martin Luther's *simul justus et peccator* (simultaneously just and sinful) embraced the paradoxical simultaneity of sin and grace. So too in business ethics, there is nothing antithetical about functioning simultaneously in both the economic world and the religious world—so long as the religious world doesn't forget that it, too, exists in part within the economic world! Or, as insightfully stated by the theologian, Edward Schillebeeckx in his book, *Jesus in Our Western Culture*, "In Jewish and Christian traditions of Faith, God is always experienced as a God concerned for humanity who always wants 'people of God' who are concerned for humanity . . ." and ". . . holiness is always contextual; it does not take place in a social vacuum. Given the present situation of suffering humanity which has now been generally recognized, political love can become the historically urgent form of contemporary holiness, the historical imperative of the moment, or in Christian terms, the present *kairos*, or moment of grace, as an appeal to all believers."

Each of us can, at the same time, be deeply committed to ethical business actions, care about the welfare of people and society, and be rewarded simultaneously for acting on both beliefs. The history of sixteenth-century Spain, during the reign of Philip II, includes a legend in which someone suggested making the impassable rivers Tajo and Manzanares navigable so as to help the impoverished in the area. The government commissar purportedly exclaimed, "No! If God so willed that those rivers should be navigable, then he would have made them so with a single word." Apparently, the government viewed the creative idea as a bold and impudent infringement on the rights of divine providence.

Let God's Fingers Do the Walking

"If God wanted it that way, he would make it so." If today's business leaders applied such an approach to the complex technical business and ideological issues of our day, then all our problems would be eradicated. What bliss humankind would enjoy if God alone would work in history. All of us could simply sit back and let God's fingers do the walking.

In the real world, however, there are those who make things happen, those who watch things happen, and those who wonder what happened. Contemporary business leaders—regardless of their religion or lack thereof, their economic bias, or their management style—know that they can create not only the destiny of their individual businesses, but also the destiny of humanity on this fragile planet. But in order to be the creators of positive destinies, they must resourcefully apply modern-day financial networks, current technology, and ethical business insights to all of their business interactions. They must have and must exercise faith and confidence in the power of the ethical economic global dynamic: if they give more, they will get back more—for themselves, their enterprises, and the global society of people. Faith of this kind and dimension gives a mature, responsible human pragmatism to those who profess a formal religion, as well as to the unchurched and the non-believer. Believers in this form of faith are not tempted to resort to a simplistic approach to divine providence and lament why God permits evil, poverty, and oppression to exist in their world. These ethical business leaders know that the power to create our future is with us here and now—the power of ethical business actions—for those who have faith!

The business ethic we envision does not exist in or create utopia. We envision a powerful business ethic that is suitable for a real world that inevitably encompasses personal and societal tragedies, suffering, and terrorism. When a cause or an ideology becomes more important than the people, then tragedies occur, people suffer, and terrorism reigns.

Although we have touched upon what we mean to be saying about faith, the topic is so important to our thesis that we want to leave no confusion whatsoever about the nature and essence of the faith that we are talking about. All too often we understand faith only in a religious context that encompasses sectarian doctrinal truths about ultimate meaning. We have no quarrel with the value of that form of faith. However, because that understanding of faith involves a specificity that shuns diversity in comprehending its faith-filled ultimate truths, only the adherents of that particular doctrine benefit. While religious faith such as that is powerful, strong, and typically unwavering, faith of that kind still has great difficulty in attaining universal acceptance as the ultimate meaning for all the diverse peoples who inhabit our pluralistic planet. There is no topic in this world around which we can expect total agreement, but nowhere is that more true than on issues of ultimate truths requiring religious faith.

Nonetheless, we can move toward a more universalizable faith if we focus our imaginations when interacting in our pluralistic political and economic worlds. We can achieve this progress, not by resorting to relativism, but rather by attending to proximate truths. Whether one believes in a personal god, a monotheistic god, a pantheistic god, or no god as the ultimate truth, the best opportunity for realizing unity is to be found in focusing on proximate truths. For instance, the idea that each person has human dignity and should therefore be given an opportunity to live a decent life is a proximate truth. Those who have faith in that proximate truth will be motivated to act with social awareness and responsibility, no matter what their ultimate belief is as to what or who endows that human dignity. This faith in proximate realities is not a second-class or inferior faith in opposition to ultimate truths. All forms of faith, whether they embrace ultimate or proximate values, have in common the characteristic that they embrace some truths that cannot be comprehended solely by rational or scientific means. The human dynamic of faith is present in the world no matter what one believes to be the ultimate meaning in life, no matter how people believe they were given that faith.

WHAT THE EXECS ARE SAYING

Bob Carlson, the former CEO and a shareholder of Reell Precision Manufacturing in suburban St. Paul, Minnesota, learned that it takes faith while literally under fire at a firebase he commanded in South Vietnam during the hellish Tet Offensive of early 1968. Carlson doesn't publicly proclaim his faith. But his experience in war and industry led him to walk the talk of ethical leadership by keeping faith with the troops.

Carlson, an army captain and engineering graduate of West Point, led a company of 150 men who fought off two consecutive nighttime attacks by a vastly superior force of North Vietnamese army troops in fierce fighting that resulted in the deaths of 150 enemy troops and one of his own. He spent two months before Tet tightening up what had been a porous, jury-rigged perimeter defense when he took command in 1967, and developing a trust with his lieutenants and enlisted GIs that became a hallmark of his business career.

Carlson, who was also nearly killed in another combat incident, was sickened by the devastation of the two-day Tet battle around his artillery base. His Vietnam experience caused the twenty-six-year-old officer to abandon plans for a military career. The highly decorated combat veteran left the army after six years in 1970.

Carlson completed an MBA from the Wharton School at the University of Pennsylvania and spent much of his career at big American companies, musing over the huge rewards accrued by many CEOs and the growing gap between them and the loyal "troops" who labored on the factory floor and research labs. He encountered tremendous cynicism toward management at several outfits where he worked in middle and senior management.

Finally, in the late 1990s, Carlson gave up working as a consultant and assumed leadership of Reell Manufacturing along with Steve Wilkstrom, the other co-CEO, and the rest of the management team. Reell was then a privately held design-and-manufacturing company established in the 1970s by three ex–3M Company engineers whose philosophy emphasized a reasonable executive compensation and rewards for hardworking, innovative employees.

In fiscal 2001, the company, which competes mostly against low-cost Asian workforces making high-tech hinges for laptop computers and automobiles, weathered a severe downturn in its core business that led to a $200,000 loss for shareholders. Rather than layoffs, Carlson, his managers, and the workers elected to take wage cuts that ranged from 16 percent among the best-paid managers to 7 percent for hourly workers. Those who made less than $11.40 per hour were exempt.

The privately held, thirty-two-year-old Reell rebounded in 2002 to a $1.5 million net profit on a more than 25 percent gain in revenue to $38 million. Wages were restored in 2002, as well as modest raises and bonuses to every worker. The company, which shares quarterly stock and financial data with all 250 employees, also granted year-end retirement and stock contributions. Moreover, in 2003 Reell was named the small-business category winner of the American Business Ethics Award given by the Society of Financial Service Professionals. The award, established in 1994, recognizes U.S. companies that exemplify high standards of ethical behavior routinely and in response to crises.

"It's a superb company, and it should serve as a role model," said Fred Zimmerman, a University of St. Thomas professor of engineering and technology management, who is also a veteran corporate manager and board member with more than thirty five years' experience. "Their ethics are integrated into their success. And there are no issues of excessive executive pay."

Reell's board of directors and top executives, including Carlson, limited themselves to pay of about $130,000—or roughly seven times that of an entry-level worker. Hourly workers at the shop can top $25 an hour. That's a contrast to many American companies, where CEOs' pay can top fifty to one hundred times that of the average worker.

Executive compensation, improved corporate governance, and living within the law are hot topics in a corporate America glutted with marquee examples of princely pay for poor performance and boardroom self-dealing. Carlson said he grew frustrated working for larger companies where he saw lip service paid to worker ideas and initiatives as executives grew richer and more distant from the workers. He attributed the rebound at Reell to a motivated sales staff and designers and workers who own a piece of the company and were ready to make the most of a business rebound.

Carlson and the other owner-managers of Reell could have lost everything if they hadn't "given" and invested in their workforce. Just as the professor learned at the outset of this chapter, your charity or sacrifice in the short term may result in a greater benefit to you and your organization downstream. Carlson's workers, most of whom are also owners, stayed on the job and helped get the company through a tough time. It took faith and short-term sacrifice from management and workers.

Carlson believed the workers delivered tremendous results for their company in 2002–03 because they were consulted and trusted by management—which chose well-spread sacrifice over layoffs to help ensure a brighter future for all the company's stakeholders. Although sickened by the ferociousness of war and combat, Carlson learned that the best commanders give of themselves, lead by example, and train and trust their troops for the best results.

Still, in 2006, Reell opened an office in China with the intention to start manufacturing some products there at the request of manufacturing companies. The Reell board, like Donaldson, intends to expand a portion of its business in China plants—while its higher-paid workforce in the United States focuses on new products, design, and next-generation manufacturing and delivery for new U.S. customers.

CONCLUSION

We are all familiar with the old axiom, "If we don't believe in something, the problem is not that we will believe in nothing, but rather that we will believe in anything." Faith is a very human response to a world filled with much that we don't know or understand. Faith helps us to embrace the pervasive mystery we experience all around our globe and permits us to live a meaningful life in spite of the doubts that are part of our every action.

None of us has all the answers and all of us have doubts as to how we should do business in our economic global society. We contend that in the global financial scenario, future prosperity is possible *only* to the degree that we can diminish the threat of terrorism and instability.

Regardless of the economic or political system within which business leaders function—be it capitalism, socialism, collectivism, or any ism—that system, that ism, is not separate from the world of suffering people. Quite the opposite, those worlds are inextricably intertwined. Business leaders, therefore, should be thoroughly ethical in their business conduct. They should not politicize their ethics, but they should "ethicize" their business involvement. Today's business leaders must stop being principled (in the ideological sense) and start doing what is right; they must start *doing ethics in business*, to borrow the apt title of a good book on this subject by Donald G. Jones.

Therefore, we add another essential ingredient to our unfolding understanding of modern-day business ethics:

Business ethics is ultimately all about faith—the faith of business leaders in their own ability to effectively and deliberately "do good and avoid evil." They must *believe* that if they give more, they will get more back for themselves, for their organizations, and for society.

Or in the words of the French philosopher Maurice Merleau-Ponty in his book *Humanism and Terror*: "Whatever one's philosophical or even theological position, a society is not the temple of value-idols that figure on the front of its monuments or in its constitutional scrolls; the value of a society is the value it places upon man's relation to man."

Take Action Questions

1. Given the idea that ethical business leaders need to respect the spiritual dimension of all people, what is the difference between religion and spirituality?

2. If a business leader proclaims to be a person of faith then must he or she also belong to a formal religion?

3. If a business leader has faith in the idea that "doing good is good" is this the same as believing ethical business practices are always good for business?

4. Should business leaders care about the dignity or fairness with which they treat their employees if employees have the freedom to find employment somewhere else if they are not satisfied?

5. Can it be demonstrated that an organization that treats its employees fairly will earn more profit? If so, how?

CHAPTER 8

Creators, Enablers, Networkers: The Role of the University

HAVING REFLECTED on the major ingredients necessary for a modern-day understanding of business ethics, we turn our attention to some instructive and critical instances in which the world of higher education intersects with the complex world of business ethics. One such well-documented situation that has, unfortunately, played itself out repetitively across the higher education landscape in recent years is the embarrassing situation in which many universities have found themselves as a result of the unethical and illegal actions of some of their more prominent and profligate benefactors.

At Seton Hall University in New Jersey, for example, faculty and students debated the merits of removing the name of ousted Tyco International Chief Executive Dennis Kozlowski from

Kozlowski Hall, the building that houses the business school at the university. Sparking the debate were criminal and civil charges brought against Kozlowski, who donated $3 million to the university between 1997 and 2000, both for having orchestrated a massive cooking of the books and for taking millions in compensation that key former Tyco board members claimed they never authorized. (After Kozlowski's conviction for grand larceny, he told university officials to remove his name from both the building and from the rotunda in the school's library.)

Disproving the maxim that lightning never strikes the same place twice, in 1995 Seton Hall faced an almost identical dilemma when its trustee and $4.75 million benefactor Robert E. Brennan, whose name graced the facade of the university's recreation center, was convicted on seven counts of bankruptcy fraud and money laundering. Students and faculty alike expressed anger at the moral implications involved with the controversy. One student said, "You can't preach morals if we are naming buildings after people that obviously aren't moral; this guy is a convicted felon." Another student opined that the university's mission was being compromised.

At the University of Missouri, the Kenneth Lay endowed chair in economics, funded with a $1.1 million gift of Enron stock from Mr. Lay, who earned undergraduate and graduate degrees from the university, stands vacant. Lay's infamy, of course, stems from the collapse of Enron Corp., the energy-trading conglomerate that dissolved into bankruptcy in 2001. Lay, Enron's CEO, was indicted for falsely promoting the company's stock and falsely stating that Enron was in good financial health, while he and other executives unloaded their own shares. Prosecutors allege he knew Enron was collapsing.

At Northwestern University's Kellogg School of Management, consternation reigned in 2001–02 as the venerable Arthur Andersen accounting firm collapsed after its criminal indictment by the U.S. Department of Justice, acting for the Securities and Exchange

Commission. Authorities concluded that Andersen partners were complicit in financial frauds that doomed investors in the likes of Enron and WorldCom.

Northwestern's administration elected not to remove the Arthur Andersen name from one of its buildings. Arthur Andersen, the man who founded the once-storied accounting firm in the early 1900s, and a generation of Andersen accountants who followed him were paragons of conservative accounting and fair play. However, as a result of its involvement in the scandals at Enron, WorldCom, and Qwest, the Arthur Andersen firm remains a symbol of the rampant corporate abuse of the late 1990s. Even though the United States Supreme Court in May 2005 reached a 9–0 decision vacating the conviction of the Arthur Andersen firm for obstruction of justice in the Enron case, the ethical condemnations of the firm remain entrenched in the public mind. And, of course, the Supreme Court "victory" was merely symbolic since the firm is essentially defunct.

In Alabama, Richard Scrushy's name adorns University of Alabama buildings and athletic fields and an entire campus at Jefferson State Community College, even though he was embroiled in accusations of financial fraud involving conduct that led to his dismissal as the top executive at HealthSouth Corp.

Each of these universities and others have wrestled with the embarrassment of being associated with now-scandalous former executives. Some must decide whether to return large sums of money and rename buildings named for now-notorious benefactors.

"Lay was CEO of an enterprise that cheated," Paul Wallace, a professor emeritus of political science at the University of Missouri, told the *Chicago Tribune* in 2003. "We feel a chair should relate to some degree of ethics. What kind of role model is he?" (Ameet Sachdev, What's a School to Do When Fallen CEOs Name on Wall?" *Chicago Tribune*, Oct. 14, 2003.) Lay, convicted former WorldCom CEO Bernie Ebbers, and the others were once considered lions of capitalism. Many are now considered cheating jackals. Did they fail their universities or did the universities fail them? We doubt they started out planning to cheat their way to millions.

Ethics Must Be Integrated into Teaching Business

Kenneth Goodpaster was founder of the business ethics program at Harvard University in the 1980s. In 2005, Goodpaster offered this analysis of the recent rash of corporate scandals:

> Take an organizational culture that is fixated on certain goals whatever the cost; combine it with the group's rationalization of its behavior in the name of those goals, and repeat this behavior again and again until the protesting consciences of the participants become detached, anesthetized. These are the symptoms of a pathology—I call it teleopathy—that can infect our most treasured institutions, including not only those in the private and public sectors but also the moral-cultural sectors of religion, the media, and education. We see these symptoms in the fanatical behavior of terrorists but we also see these symptoms in the obsessive behavior of corporate executives. (Goodpaster, "Conscience and Corporate Culture," *B* [spring 2005]: 18–21.)

Goodpaster believes that this disturbing trend predates the stock market boom of the 1990s. He traces the roots of this malaise to Ivan Boesky, the insider trader jailed in the 1980s, and the bad actors behind the Salomon Brothers bond scandals of the same decade, and even to the corporate thieves of earlier times.

"Fixation. Rationalization. Detachment." writes Goodpaster. "These are symptoms of a hazard to which both individuals and groups can succumb. Objectives become idols; obstacles become threats; second thoughts are not allowed—and eventually, second thoughts disappear. Despite the behavior of individual decision makers, the larger reality is a cultural reality, and this viewpoint has been characteristic of diagnosis after diagnosis of corporate wrongdoing in recent years."

Goodpaster, in a recent article, cites Warren Bennis, distinguished professor of business administration at the University of Southern California's Marshall School of Business, who wrote about Ken Lay's role in Enron's collapse in the February 17, 2002, edition of the *New York Times*: "Mr. Lay's failing is not simply his myopia or cupidity or incompetence, it is his inability to create a company culture open to reality, one that does not discourage managers from delivering bad news. No organization can be honest with the public if it is not honest with itself."

Goodpaster and Bennis advance the perspective that the obsessive drive of corporate leaders to please Wall Street analysts and shareholders by hitting or exceeding financial projections—and the allure of the resulting seven-figure paydays—can and does lead some executives to stray incrementally into unethical and illegal behavior.

Goodpaster maintains that if we are to avoid defaulting on the moral formation of future leaders, ethics must be integrated into the teaching of business in the academy. He also writes of the Third Academy, comprised of associations of business, academic, and civic leaders who establish and monitor global standards. One stellar example of the Third Academy is the Caux Round Table, an international association of businesses and business leaders who subscribe to and promote voluntary ethical practices. Another is Saint Mary's University of Minnesota's Hendrickson Institute for Ethical Leadership and its Fellows Program, in which business executives convene to discuss and grapple with ever-changing contemporary ethical business issues and challenges.

Small wonder, in the wake of the corporate ethics scandals, that there's a buzz of activity at ethics laboratories from the Wharton School at the University of Pennsylvania to the Stanford

University Business School in California. Bravo! It's never too late to learn, to teach, and to start doing ethics. These universities and others must work tirelessly to create the next generation of leaders, women and men who will walk the walk of long-term interest on behalf of the balanced stakeholder interests of owners, employees, and host communities. If the ethical report card of the next generation of leaders is as abysmal as the rap sheet of some of the discredited leaders we have mentioned above, the decades ahead will again find universities struggling with how to "spin" their relationships with alumni and other benefactors whose names have become synonymous with amorality, greed, and other malfeasances.

So, what can the academy do to make sure our universities never have to deal with the dilemma of renaming a building or returning money from an unethical benefactor? Or, more importantly, how can universities transform themselves into more effective teachers of doing ethics in business?

Simple answer: teach students to do ethics. The not-so-simple challenge: how to do that. In the present scandal-laced environment of business, the public is probably disinclined to grant our universities high grades as effective teachers of business ethics. It is much more likely that an increasingly cynical and agitated public wonders why the most egregious of the well-known highly unethical business leaders have their names on buildings and endowed professorial chairs at public and private universities.

Rugged Individualism?

Reasonable people accept reality. We can't achieve perfection! Reasonable people, while valuing the cultural, social, and economic blessings and opportunities inherent in capitalism, also understand that at its wretched excess, the rewards of capitalism for some at the top of the corporate pyramid are, by any standard, disproportionate and unjustifiable. Inevitably, the temptation of such rewards inspires a small minority to cheat.

The traditional American culture, throughout more than two centuries, has adopted and glorified an ethos in which rugged individualism is desired and admired. Our culture is increasingly skewed toward an ethic of the individual conscience. To some degree, academia reflects this ethos with its teachings and respect for entrepreneurship, its endorsement of the heroic American entrepreneur who mortgages the home *and* firstborn to finance a dream that one day becomes millions of dollars for the courageous, daring, visionary founder who risked everything. But, in reality, most college graduates go on to work for collective organizations known as corporations. They take entry-level or professional jobs. And some rise to the top.

As president for twenty-one years (1984–2005) of Saint Mary's University of Minnesota, a Lasallian Catholic university, and as a successful entrepreneur in the 1960s before he entered the DeLaSalle Christian Brothers, a Roman Catholic teaching order, Brother Louis DeThomasis understood the need to lace our teachings about the rugged individualism of capitalism with discussion of the societal benefits attendant to creating a common ground for stakeholders that is not vulnerable to unilateral exploitation by a rogue CEO driven by power and greed. Though quite proud and impressed by Saint Mary's University of Minnesota's proactive and dynamic commitment to develop strong, competent, ethical business leaders, all of its leaders—administration, faculty, staff, and trustees—wanted to make an even more substantial impact in this regard. This commitment to teaching students about ethical business is not just within the purview of religiously affiliated institutions of higher learning. Jeffrey E. Garten, the outgoing ten-year dean of the Yale School of Management, has expressed parallel interests and motivations. Garten, a thirteen-year veteran of Wall Street and a former undersecretary of commerce for international trade, cannot be dismissed as an ivory tower, out-of-touch academician, with no experience in the trenches. Reflecting on his tenure at Yale, Garten said, "I had hoped when I came here there would be a great interest among the faculty and the students in producing business leaders who first and foremost would run profitable organizations, but who also would have some involvement in creating a more prosperous and equitable world economy," *New York Times*, June 19, 2005. He added that although he was not frustrated he still harbored an important, yet unanswered, question, namely, "Is it possible to produce MBA graduates who will not only be greater leaders of their companies but also make a much broader contribution to the world economy and the society at large? The formula for doing that has still to be invented."

But invent we must! More than ever, the equation for successful business in a global economy includes an essential and integral role for universities. Business today finds itself embedded in a world of technology, complexity, and sophistication unparalleled both in its scope and in its transitory tenure. Even the many great leaps and technological epiphanies in the history of our economic worlds leave us without precedent or tools to deal with the incredibly brief shelf life and unimaginable convolution of technological breakthroughs today. Because American higher education can forge ahead from a position of strength, and because our universities are blessed with thousands upon thousands of competent and dedicated faculty and staff members, we must expect, indeed demand, that our universities respond with energy, enthusiasm, and commitment to our call for them to reinvent and re-create themselves—now!

A GLOBAL FOCUS—A NECESSITY

The challenge is global! The task is vital and can't be ignored—do ethical business or do business as usual and watch the disintegration of global economic potential. It is not an overstatement to proclaim for all to hear that for the peoples and nations of the world to survive economic ethical dynamics must thrive. We need the commitment of our universities to partner with business to educate the next generations of ethical business leaders and workers.

- Our universities must recognize the compelling reality that is our world of competing economies.
- Our universities must be global educational leaders.
- Our universities must educate and prepare our students to be ethical global business leaders and workers.
- Our universities must give their students the skills to orchestrate and participate in global economic success.
- Our universities must achieve all these goals while concurrently inspiring students to do ethical business that will benefit all on our globe.

Dean Garten captured the essence of this mandate when he spoke of his vision for "a global school that matches a global market." However, he added, "No business school is even close to approaching that degree of global focus."

Though this book is not the forum to deal with the details of just how our universities can reinvent themselves, we do present a vision as to what effective higher education should look like if it is to be an effective instrument in keeping the U.S. national economy vital and our business interests sustaining profitability while doing ethics in our global society.

We must reinvent our universities. Our global educational needs can no longer be satisfied by a university that is just an "academy," comprised of learned, tenured professors who develop curricula that embody the knowledge to be imparted and who guide research for the attainment of new knowledge. Quality curricula and productive research are important and essential, and the foundations for quality and excellence in higher education. However effective education for our global society and economies must transcend not only the walls of academic buildings and campuses, but even more importantly, the "walls" of educational biases built up over the decades, walls that exist and flourish in the minds of many educators, especially business school educators.

NOT INFORMATION, BUT IN FORMATION

No longer can our universities and business schools envision themselves as the dispensers of information in business and business ethics. Our universities and business schools require nothing less than a transformation! Instead of dispensers of information, educators must become the *creators, enablers,* and *networkers* of business ethics, "in formation"! The substance and spirit of business ethics cannot be covered in a smattering of elective course offerings; we must form our students by integrating ethics into every course and every internship until it becomes nothing short of second nature. Whether individuals occupy a seat in the front row of the classroom or on the executive row of the corporation, they must learn to consider—and how to consider—the ethical implications of every business case or business decision that comes before them. They must be formed to integrate attention to ethical implications so fully into their decision-making process that without hesitation they can consider a complex situation and assess the extent to which their options will comply with the law, and will adversely or positively affect the entire range of stakeholders, and will pass their mother's "smell test."

Let us first consider the role of higher education as *creator* of a business ethic. This *new* business ethic must specifically countermand the prevailing business environment that permits the free market to exercise power over an individual's most basic principles and values. In no way do we advocate rejection of American capitalism and the free market society in which so many live and prosper. An ethic that rejects those principles would devastate the moral and political freedoms that are at the core of our societal strength. In his 1960s book *Capitalism and Freedom*, Milton Friedman, the eminent economist, demonstrated quite convincingly that the free market's direct benefit to society is its protection of the freedoms of speech, religion, and thought. So, when we seek to advance an ethic that we say is counter to the free market, we are not suggesting that the principle of the free market be discarded; instead we are promoting a free market milieu in which our basic principles and values affect conduct in the marketplace, instead of the market overriding our principles and values. The business ethic we envision will not weaken the free market system; it will strengthen, advance, and perpetuate the practice of a form of capitalism that is profitable, stakeholder-oriented, and ethical.

University business programs should not simply engage in intellectual gyrations that give the appearance of effecting solutions for hypothetical or real problems; rather, they must provide leadership in the creation of an integrated ethical process, an ethical consciousness that will permeate the entire curriculum of the college, not just that of the business department. In traditional academic courses, such as Introduction to Philosophy 101 or Ethics 101, not enough is done to move students toward understanding of a viable and comprehensive business ethic. We believe that business ethics must be integrated into every fiber of university curricula in general and business curricula in particular.

Let's learn from our losses and the pain inflicted by some of our formerly famous and now infamous alumni! Creating an effective process that changes the marketplace for the better requires an interdisciplinary approach to developing, researching, and studying a business ethic. The process must spring from a multifaceted pedagogy that welcomes student input and respects and considers the needs and perspectives of the business community; only with openness to a range of ideas can universities fulfill the mandate to create something new, something more than the knowledge and perspectives that the professor presents to the students.

Traditional higher education methodologies for teaching business ethics often focus on individualistic themes: respect for private property, personal honesty, the honoring of contracts, and employee loyalty. In recent decades, we have observed that this ostrich approach to the challenges inherent in business ethics has been rendered somewhat impotent by the powerful and compelling issues brought forward by women and minorities, unions, activist shareholders, and host communities.

The fine research of Jean Piaget and Lawrence Kohlberg supports our premise that ethical behavior can be taught and developed by the university. Kohlberg's six stages of moral development clearly demonstrate how a person can progress from the first stage of responding to punishment and rewards to the final stage of acting upon principle at any cost. It is in that last stage that we will observe people engaged in *doing* ethics in business.

We also look to the university as the *enabler* for doing ethics in business. To fulfill this essential role, the university must purge itself of the traditional business ethics perspectives that embody an unproductive tension between academia and business. The tension finds its roots in the premises postulated by some that the corporation is solely a creation of the state or solely an instrument of its owners. In fact, the corporation is both. The corporation must be seen as part of the community, not as an entity in competition with or opposed to the community. Despite the protestations of some, there is nothing about corporations that is inherently bad or negative.

We subscribe to the notion that the corporation is an association of persons, workers, and owners. Its existence derives from the will of those persons who created the corporation and staff it. The corporation is subservient to the law and is granted a legal charter to operate in the public interest.

Owners and management, based on their education and experiences, shape the behavior of the corporation. Because the university often plays an influential role in the development of the perspectives and values of business leaders, it enjoys a unique opportunity to effect corporate commitments to ethical behavior. It is in the university that tomorrow's leaders can and should learn critical thinking skills related to profits and losses, research and development, finance, marketing, and the entire gamut of business challenges—including ethical challenges and the implications of business decisions and actions on the corporation's stakeholders. Too often, however, we see universities abdicate their role as enablers of ethical business because of their fear or disparagement of business or business executives.

Finally, we come to the university's role as networker. For many years now, *networking* has been a buzzword for using personal connections as a vehicle first for finding a job through acquaintances of business acquaintances, and subsequently for achieving business success. We believe that universities should creatively research and teach about a "network" that interweaves profit motivation, sensitivity, liberation from poverty, and the freedom of human action. After all, capitalism only truly works when it liberates the masses from poverty. Just making the boss rich doesn't fulfill the tenets of faith of all the great religions—or create a sustainable business model.

MIND SHARE PLUS HEART SHARE EQUALS MARKET SHARE

Look at the "crony capitalism" in places like the Philippines and Latin America, where 90 percent of the people own almost nothing and work for slave wages. Capitalism there only works for a small percentage of people. Imagine the larger market and greater profits that would be created if the vast majority of workers made a decent living wage.

Today we observe with concern that the gap between the wealthy and the working class in America is growing. Why is this so? How is it that so many are blind to the reality that ethical capitalism must be used to better enrich the workers as well as those who control capital? Workers must have a realistic expectation that they can better themselves and their families. Again, imagine the larger market and greater profits that would be created in the United States if more workers made a better living wage. Capitalism cannot just be for those who control the capital if we want more profits for our businesses and our economy.

In 1988, Minneapolis-based Norwest Corporation acquired San Francisco–based Wells Fargo & Co., and assumed the Wells Fargo name. Norwest's CEO, Stanford-educated Richard Kovacevich, became chairman and CEO of the newly merged entity, which—over the last decade—has become one of America's five largest and best-performing banking companies. Kovacevich long ago concluded—and proclaimed to securities analysts, among others—that employees are his most important stakeholders. Most executives still list stockholders. Kovacevich essentially said, "If employees aren't satisfied and motivated, the customers won't be served and we may lose them. That's not good for long-term shareholders."

Wells Fargo is one of the few companies in America to grow employment and business in the wake of a merger. Kovacevich and his leadership team believe in internal promotion, and retraining and placement elsewhere of employees instead of layoffs. He wrote recently, "Because we believe in people as our competitive advantage, we'll continue to invest in our 'human capital.' It's the most important, valuable investment we can make." He concluded his remarks by referring to a core tenet of the Wells Fargo corporate culture: "Our formula for greatness starts and ends with people: 'Mind share plus heart share equals market share,'" (Kovacevich, "Vision and Values," https: www.wellsfargo.com/invest_relations/ vision_values/).

For Richard Kovacevich and other leaders like him, the highest priority—among many competing demands—is doing the right thing, not focusing on the analyst-pleasing, short-term profitable option. Kovacevich is a millionaire many times over. He has a most comfortable seat atop the capitalist pyramid. He has also created working class–to–upper class jobs for thousands of employees who support families on Wells Fargo paychecks. Kovacevich is not perfect. A case can be made that he and other executives are grossly overpaid. He was the fifth highest-paid CEO in America in 2004 at $73 million, albeit 90 percent of his wealth accrues through improved performance of the company and the stock price for all shareholders. Still, it's hard to swallow tens of millions for big bankers in a business of high turnover for $9-per-hour tellers who can't afford the rent.

Yet educators need to study and then share with their students the success stories of enlightened capitalists who "democratize capitalism" by sharing the rewards of success with everyone, from directors in the boardroom to employees in the mailroom. Kovacevich did it. Under his leadership, for fifteen years, every Wells Fargo employee has gotten stock options. Everyone has an incentive to increase the performance and profits of the company. And those positive returns benefit the employees with a higher stock price.

It is truly amazing—and quite distressing—that there are those among us, including some in the academy, who continue to buy the premise that Marxism and Communism accord the worker loftier status and more equitable treatment than capitalism. The naked truth is that Marxism and Communism don't work to benefit workers any more than any other form of tyranny. Martin Marty, distinguished Lutheran scholar and emeritus professor at the University of Chicago, succinctly addresses this point: "The communisms and socialisms failed utterly to produce economic equality in the systems where these were related to authoritarian government." We need only look at Stalin's Soviet Union, Mao's cultural revolution in China, and Pol Pot's Cambodian reign of terror to prove our point.

Theologian Rafael Belda has succinctly emphasized the necessity of an ethical system that goes beyond an attempt to achieve mere materialistic equality for all humans:

> Man's moral task does have a radical religious meaning, for human action concurs with God's plan of liberation. But fulfilling moral law does not mean surrendering human creativity to the caprice of a despot. It rather means fidelity to the ethical exigencies which build the human person in human community. Man, a social and historical being, discovers, by trial and error, the law that channels his human growth. Thus, natural moral law is imminent (to individual and social structures) and transcendent (expressing God's creative and liberation plan). A grasp of Christian ethics that is faithful to the gospel shows that a right pursuit of God's command must issue in commitment to changing the world. Christian love has a social-political dimension. (Rafael Belda, "Christian Reflection on Marxist Ethic," *Theology Digest* [Spring 1979].)

The social, economic, moral, and cultural dynamics of the college and university comprise networks that provide the basis for an integrated business ethic, one that can affect the attitudes of academicians, students, and businesspeople nationwide. We need to broaden the network to all universities, for it is within these universities that we create successive generations of artists, scientists, and businesspeople. We do not advocate invading the academy with pious groups of religious zealots. They can be dangerous, too. We suggest advancing the ethical practice of doing the right thing on behalf of long-term stakeholders as a curricular component every bit as important as the fundamental business courses. Of course, creativity abounds in the university, so these "ethics networks" come in many and various shapes and forms. One model does not fit all.

The University of Pennsylvania's Wharton School of Business has embraced this concept by incorporating business ethics into a dozen graduate courses, including accounting, marketing, and finance.

Reporter Ronald Alsop reported in the *Wall Street Journal* ("MBA Track," April 12, 2005) on efforts at the Columbia University Business School to infuse ethics into the business curriculum. Professional actors stage "Scenes from a Slippery Slope," a short work in which a businessman is pressured to falsify expense accounts to conceal his boss's extramarital affair. At pivotal points during the short production, Columbia Business School students are called upon to advise the businessperson as he works through his ethical dilemma.

Duke University's Fuqua School of Business demonstrated that teaching business ethics can be a messy process sometimes. In 2004, Fuqua MBA students staged a mock trial of their business program. The verdict: "Fuqua, one of the nation's premier B-school programs, was failing to teach the tenets of corporate leadership," according to *Business Week*. "With only one required course on ethics or leadership and a code of conduct with too few penalties for violations, the Duke program, students concluded, inadequately prepared them to be ethical business leaders" (Jennifer Merritt, *Business Week*, Oct. 18, 2004). "The bummer of what we learned is that Team Fuqua promotes not holding each other accountable," said Amy Pierce, a second-year student.

In the same *Business Week* article, Merritt describes how the University of Maryland's Robert H. Smith School of Business has put ethics in a real-life context by arranging a "field trip" in which second-year MBA students visited white-collar inmates—people convicted of securities fraud, money laundering, and embezzlement—in federal prisons. "Their backgrounds were so similar to ours and they did jobs we are going to be doing," said Kevon Kothari, a 2004 Maryland MBA now employed by Intel. If learning experiences like these don't enable students to network, little will.

From every corner of higher education in America—from the Stanford School of Business to Dartmouth's Amos Tuck, and from the McCombs School of Business at the University of Texas to the University of Michigan's Ross School of Business—universities are connecting, building strong and integrated networks, no longer studying either business or ethics in unconnected academic silos. Instead, we see these leading universities studying the theory and application of ethical organizations, integrating ethics education and discussions across and throughout the curriculum, and then sharing what they are doing with their alumni and with other schools. That's enabling! That's creating! That's networking! And it's all good. If our universities will build on this momentum, they will individually and collectively avoid the shame and embarrassment of trying to disassociate themselves from alumni whose unethical and criminal behavior taints all with whom they have had contact.

What the Execs Are Saying

Nick Moore, the retired CEO of the accounting firm PricewaterhouseCoopers, doesn't claim to be an education expert, although he's lectured at Notre Dame and other prestigious business schools. He does know business schools can do a better job of emphasizing ethics as well as discounting cash flows.

"The folks going to Harvard and Stanford were going there to hone their business skills but were probably less focused on developing a moral compass," said the California-based Moore. "It is important for these schools to drill down to the ethical issues arising from business and to use guest lecturers who've been there, if the professors haven't."

Exactly. Business schools generally have focused too much on making a buck, counting the buck, and investing the bucks. They need to focus more on how the buck is made and the concept of stakeholder value. It is written in the Old Testament that "the temple stands unfinished until all are housed in dignity." No businessperson is really an ethical capitalist unless employees are fairly compensated, commitments are honored—and all profits are made fairly.

Bob Kierlin, the chairman of Fastenal, believes we'd be a more ethical business community if "more of our young people went to religious-based schools." He's not advocating state-supported Christian academies by any stretch of the imagination. But Kierlin believes a lot of families and public schools have failed to stress the morality and personal ethics necessary to create solid citizens and businesspeople. In fact, Kierlin said business schools often focus too much on technical matters and not enough on empowering creativity and innovation in the ranks—a hallmark of his company.

"Everyone has their own character, instilled by families, friends, and school," he said. "And that's what people bring to work with them. There isn't much you can do after they are an adult. We fire about 10 people a year out of 8,400 employees for unethical behavior, such as falsifying records or overstating commissions. That's not a lot."

Meanwhile, maybe all the executive scandals of recent years and subsequent focus in business schools and otherwise is starting to resonate with the next generation. The number of teenagers who say they would act unethically to get ahead if there were *no chance* of getting caught has dropped to 22 percent in 2005 from 33 percent in 2003, according to a recent poll by Junior Achievement and Deloitte & Touche, another of the Big Four accounting firms.

However, while exhibiting a strong sense of ethical principles, many teens don't have the courage to maintain their convictions under pressure: more than 40 percent of those polled said they might act unethically if instructed by their boss and more than a third said they would likely lie to their boss to cover up a mistake at work. "The need to conduct business honestly is a message that we must instill in our future business leaders," said Jon Eisele, a managing partner at Deloitte. "The survey results are telling us that there is a need for ethics education."

Deloitte and Junior Achievement have joined to expand ethics education with the JA programs for young people in the fourth grade through high school. "The survey findings, regrettably, are consistent with what we're seeing in the workplace," said Arthur Brief, director of the Burkenroad Institute for the Study of Ethical Leadership at Tulane University. "Without education and a culture that encourages ethical behavior, sometimes good people can make bad decisions."

Paul Meyer, the chief executive of Clear Channel Outdoor, ticked off a list of instances where advertising agencies or officials of foreign governments have asked for bribes described as "commissions," "fees," or otherwise.

"The first time I see anything like that, we go straight to the client to lay it out," said Meyer, a graduate of Notre Dame Law School. "In the end, I don't want that kind of business. It puts good business at risk.

"I suspect that business schools don't place enough emphasis on ethics. It's shocking to me. I've had to fire employees for ethical improprieties. People rationalize their behavior. Ethics are fundamental. They are universal. And they need to be taught as universal truths."

Conclusion

Universities and business schools must form their students with the knowledge and skills necessary for them to become the leaders, managers, and executives of efficient and profitable organizations. Concurrently, those same students must also acquire knowledge and understanding of their obligation to help create and sustain a prosperous and equitable world economy. Not only does this make good ethical sense, but, just as important, it also makes eminently good business sense. This ethically powerful principle of a prosperous world economy benefits all people on this globe. At the same time, it generates enormous business dividends that propel the free enterprise engine to produce more and more profits through the creation of ever-expanding markets.

It pays to do ethics in business. Have faith!

Now we have come to our final ingredient in our attempt to explain the complex components of business ethics:

In their finest moments, universities awaken, nurture, and empower learners to ethical lives of service and leadership. The leaders we educate today will determine the culture of tomorrow's corporations. If that culture is to be ethical and have as its core objective the profitable expansion of markets for all the people of the globe, universities must remove business ethics from its academic silo and fully integrate a pragmatic approach to doing business ethics throughout the curriculum.

Take Action Questions

1. Can universities and business schools really "teach" business ethics to students?

2. Should business take a much greater interest and work directly with universities in developing curriculum?

3. Should universities take gift money from businesspeople or businesses who are not respected for their ethical business practices?

4. Should business leaders feel compelled to find direct ways that they could be part of universities and business schools' mission to teach students?

5. Should universities and business schools be more proactive in working with businesses in teaching business ethics?

CHAPTER 9

If They See It,
They Will Have It

THE FINAL SENTENCE of this book's first chapter says: "In this book, we will attempt to move the dialogue in the direction of a globally acceptable understanding by coming up with a pragmatic, effective, and meaningful definition of the term *business ethics*." Have we fulfilled that promise?

Especially in view of the abundant, misguided, quick-fix approaches to business ethics, a globally acceptable understanding necessarily incorporates two elements. The less important of these is to understand what business ethics is not, which we hope we have effectively demonstrated. Business ethics is not

- applying the simplistic solutions of the past to the complex realities of our global economic system;

- doing nothing more than adhering to the tenets of codes of ethics, acting in accordance with business laws, and ensuring compliance with governmental regulations;

- expecting religion, the academy, or any other entity to provide the single right answer to every ethical conundrum that emerges; or

- being ethical.

The more important element in a globally acceptable understanding of business ethics is to identify the ingredients required for the business leader to successfully navigate the treacherous waters of global commerce. We believe that we have made a strong case for inclusion of the following ingredients:

- An attitude that embraces differences and ambiguity (for the world is overflowing with both)

- Appreciation for the gift of diverse cultures, including our own

- Creative imagination that leads not to change, but to transformation

- A new language of stewardship and abundance that transcends ideology

- Acceptance of and enthusiasm for the positive integration of faith and finance

- An unwavering commitment to do good and to give more

- Faith that the certain outcome of giving more is that we get more for our organizations, for ourselves, and for all of humankind

- Universities, around the globe, that create, enable, and network ethical business leaders

- Doing ethics!

Those are the ingredients. What about a recipe? The *Oxford English Dictionary* (OED) defines *recipe* as "a formula for the composition or use of a remedy, a prescription," and as "a statement of the ingredients and procedure required for making something, especially a dish in cookery." A typical kitchen recipe will prescribe a specific preset oven temperature, a precise quantity for each ingredient, the order in which the ingredients are to be added, and a directive as to how long the dish needs to be cooked.

If we were to suggest a recipe—one recipe—for our ingredients, we would be repeating the very behaviors and perspectives we have harshly criticized in these pages. While we have great confidence that the application of our ingredients will and does generate the pragmatic, effective, and meaningful answer we promised, we posit with equal conviction that the business leader doing ethical business will creatively mix the ingredients in varying amounts and in varying sequences over varying spans of time, depending on the circumstances, consequences, and stakeholder interest in each unique situation. *If they see it, they will have it.*

This point is central to our premise. A pragmatic answer, by definition (again, according to the OED), is one that is suited for and leads to action, "as opposed to theoretical or idealistic" speculation. Action! *Doing* ethics!

While all of the ingredients we have suggested are essential for doing ethics in business, one stands as a prerequisite for all the others, and that is imagination. Albert Einstein said, "Imagination is more important than knowledge." Imagination distinguishes the leader from the manager. The combination of imagination and faith enables a leader to make sound decisions even when faced with unknown and unknowable variables. Without imagination, business leaders cannot create the new language, embrace ambiguity, or comprehend the synergy between faith and finance.

The business leader—blessed with an unfettered imagination and the vision to study ethical challenges and calculate the appropriate quantity and sequence and mix of the ingredients we have suggested—can *do* business ethics. Just as important, the leader's ethical decisions and actions will not only bring meaningful success to the business and to its numerous stakeholders, but will also have positive consequences for the global community in which all businesses operate. *If they see it, they will have it.*

> Do not follow where the path may lead.
> Go instead where there is no path and leave a trail.
>
> — *Unknown*

Take Action Question

Now it's your turn: How do you do your part to balance ethics and profits in your organization?

Contributors

Brad Anderson

The CEO of Best Buy, Brad Anderson, is a native of Sheridan, Wyoming. He has an associate's degree from Waldorf College and a bachelor's degree from the University of Denver. He began his career in 1973 as a commissioned salesman when Best Buy was a single store in St. Paul called Sound of Music. He claims he took the job so he could get paid for listening to music and was known, as a salesman, to drive to customers' homes to help install the equipment for free.

Twenty-nine years later, he became the chief executive officer of Best Buy. Through his innovative leadership, since 2002 Best Buy has been the leading U.S. consumer-electronics specialty retailer, employing nearly 120,000 employees and serving close to 30 million customers daily with more than 900 retail locations spanning the United States and Canada, and with recent plans for expansion into China. And to think, he just wanted to get paid to listen to music.

Bob Carlson

Bob Carlson is the former co-CEO of Reell Precision Manufacturing, which is known for its development and production of friction hinges and precision springs and wrap-spring clutches used in laptop computers, power tools, copiers, and automobiles. Reell had over $36 million in sales in 2003 and more than 225 employees internationally. Carlson and others who have been part of the Reell team have a long history of ethical leadership and profitable business, winning many state and national awards for their remarkable ethical philosophy. Reell was one of three Minnesota companies out of 160 nominated for the 2002 Minnesota Business Ethics Award by the Society of Financial Service Professionals (SFSP), which recognizes high standards of ethical behavior. A couple of years later, SFSP awarded Carlson an ethics award on a national level.

Bob Carlson is an engineering graduate of the U.S. Military Academy at West Point, a combat veteran of Vietnam, and a graduate of the prestigious Wharton School of Economics.

Janet Dolan

Seventeen years after her 1989 appointment, Janet Dolan retired as president and CEO of Tennant Company in 2006. Janet began providing her leadership skills to Tennant in 1986 and held several positions from associate general counsel to executive vice president. Tennant Company manufactures nonresidential floor-maintenance equipment, floor coatings, and related products. During her years as CEO, the company expanded into commercial and outdoor markets with reported sales of $126 million in 2005.

Janet's career began as an attorney for Southern Minnesota Regional Legal Services, where she became assistant director of the Minnesota Lawyers' Professional Responsibility Board in 1980. She has a BA from the College of Saint Catherine and a law degree from William Mitchell College of Law.

Dolan remains very active, serving on the boards of Donaldson Company, Inc., The St. Paul Travelers Companies, Inc., and the Greater Twin Cities United Way. She is the chairwoman of the Minnesota Business Partnership and a member of the NYSE Listed Company Advisory Committee.

Janet is also the recipient of the 2005 Tekne Award for Established Leadership in recognition of her strong leadership skills as CEO of Tennant Company and in the greater community. She is known for her ability to generate new ideas, her positive encouragement, and her commitment to leadership by example.

Robert Kierlin

Current chairman of the board and past president and CEO (as of 2001) Robert (Bob) Kierlin started the Fastenal Company in 1967. Over the past thirty years, Fastenal has become the fastest-growing full-line industrial distributor and largest fastener distributor in the nation with twelve distribution centers in the United States, including a fleet of more than 275 company-owned semitrucks and trailers and more than 1,700 store sites located in every state in the United States, Canada, Mexico, the Dominican Republic, Puerto Rico, and Singapore.

Bob Kierlin is known and appreciated for his fiscal frugality from when he halved his conservative $130,000 Fastenal salary as a result of his time-consuming duties as a Republican state senator (elected in 1999). He has never been known to receive a bonus, or restrict shares or stock options since Fastenal went public in 1987.

Kierlin graduated with a Bachelor of Mechanical Engineering degree from the University of Minnesota, where he also completed his master's in business administration. He currently resides in Winona, Minnesota, and serves on several business boards and advisory boards of the University of Minnesota.

Paul Meyer

Prior to his appointment as CEO of Clear Channel Outdoor worldwide operations, a division of Clear Channel Communications, Paul Meyer was the president and CEO of Clear Channel Outdoor's North and Latin American division. He serves as the elected chairman of the Outdoor Advertising Association of America. He also serves on the board of directors and the executive committee of the Traffic Audit Bureau and is its secretary and treasurer, as well as a member of a number of boards of nonprofit organizations.

Clear Channel Outdoor, based in Phoenix, Arizona, is a global leader in outdoor advertising with over 800,000 displays in more than fifty countries worldwide. The company operates over 164,000 advertising displays and has a significant presence in forty-two U.S. markets, including displays in Times Square, on over 45,000 taxis in the United States, in approximately two hundred shopping malls, and in fifteen major U.S. airports and forty-one international airports. Clear Channel Outdoor began doing business as Foster & Kleiser Outdoor Advertising in 1901, the original pioneers in outdoor advertising, and eventually in 1997 became a wholly owned subsidiary of Clear Channel Communications, one of the world's largest media companies.

Paul obtained his undergraduate degree, summa cum laude, from St. Mary's University of Minnesota and later received his law degree, cum laude, from the University of Notre Dame, where he was the editor in chief of the Notre Dame Law Review. Before entering private practice as an attorney, he served as senior law clerk to Chief Justice Earl Warren of the Unites States Supreme Court and then served for over twenty years as the managing partner of Meyer, Hendricks & Bivens and its predecessor law firms. In 2002, he received an honorary doctorate degree in Ethical Leadership from Saint Mary's University in recognition of his outstanding ethical leadership.

Nicholas Moore

Nicholas Moore is the retired global chairman of Pricewaterhouse-Coopers and CEO of the U.S. firm, one of the world's top accounting firms since the 1998 merger between Coopers and Lybrand and Price Waterhouse. He was elected chairman and CEO of Coopers and Lybrand in 1994 and chairman and CEO of Coopers and Lybrand International in 1997. He currently serves on the board of directors of Bechtel Group, Inc.; Wells Fargo Bank; Gilead Sciences, Inc.; Network Appliance; and certain private venture capital–backed technology companies. He has provided his business leadership skills as chairman of the board of trustees of Saint Mary's College of California and is a member of the American Institute of CPAs, the California Bar Association, and the California and New York Society of CPAs. Moore received his BS in accounting from Saint Mary's College of California and later received his JD from Hastings College of Law, University of California. He is known to frequently share his vast business knowledge and leadership experience as a guest speaker for business groups, colleges, and universities throughout the country.

Brother Michael O'Hern, FSC

President and CEO of Christian Brothers Investment Services, Inc. (CBIS), Brother Michael O'Hern, FSC, also serves on its board of directors. Prior to his appointment as CEO, he served as executive vice president, during which time he contributed significantly to the growth and success of CBIS. Under his leadership, CBIS has become the world's leading investment management firm focusing on socially responsible investing for Catholic institutions and is in the top half of all money managers worldwide, with over $4 billion in assets serving over one thousand institutional Catholic clients across the globe.

CBIS was founded in 1981 by the De La Salle Christian Brothers to provide trusted socially responsible investment management services exclusively for Catholic organizations. Brother O'Hern's strategic insight and vision has effectively carried out this mission, focusing on top issues such as sweatshops, militarism, human rights, global warming, and AIDS.

Brother O'Hern graduated with a BA from Lewis University, received an MBA from the University of Chicago, an MA in Administration from Northwestern University, and an MA in history from Michigan State University. Prior to his service at CBIS, Brother O'Hern was a school system administrator in the Archdiocese of Chicago, which provided him insight into the investment needs and challenges facing Catholic organizations.

Tom Petters

Current chairman and CEO of Petters Group Worldwide Tom Petters began a trading company in the late 1980s with minimal to no capital. During his sixteen years of leadership, Petters Group Worldwide has grown from a small business into a successful organization with over 3,200 employees reaching around the globe. Petters Group Worldwide is a privately held investment company with a collection of over twenty-six public and private companies focused in manufacturing, partnerships, technology, and brands. Familiar names to the consumer include Polaroid, uBid Inc., and Fingerhut Global offices, which are located in the United States, South America, Asia, and Europe.

Tom Petters, born and raised in St. Cloud, Minnesota, is a recognized leader in his field and known for his creativity and innovation. To a diverse group of charities and universities he is known for his generosity with time, money, and energy. Tom serves on the board of trustees at the College of St. Benedict and Rollins College and on the Business Advisory Council for Richard T. Farmer

School of Business at Miami of Ohio. He has donated millions of dollars to Miami University to establish a study center in memory of his son, John, and to Rollins College, where his daughter attended, to endow a new faculty chair in the department of International Business. Tom financially and personally supports partnerships with a number of universities where he believes the opportunity for international education through the Petters China Learning Center will benefit students and faculty from many campuses. He has backed Collegeville, Minnesota communities—lifelong learning communities aimed at providing seniors educational opportunities. His leadership and generosity can be seen around the globe.

Warren Staley

The chief executive officer of Cargill since 1999, Warren Staley was elected chairman of the board in 2000 and was the chairman of the Cargill Foundation until December 2005. He is the former head of Cargill in Argentina. He shares his leadership skills with the board of directors of U.S. Bancorp, Target Corporation, and in the past has served the Greater Twin Cities United Way, and the Minnesota Private Colleges Council. Staley's Midwestern roots reach from his hometown of Springfield, Illinois, and Kansas State University in Manhattan, Kansas, where he received a BA in electrical engineering. He later received an MBA from Cornell University.

Under his leadership, Cargill generated over $71 billion in revenue in 2005; became ranked number one on the Forbes Private 500; employs more than 97,000 people in fifty-nine countries including Brazil, Egypt, and Venezuela; and has been actively involved in agri-business with China.

Selected Bibliography

Belda, Rafael. "Christian Reflection on Marxian Ethic." *Theology Digest*, 27, no.1, p. 25. (Spring, 1979): 25.

Benedict, Ruth. *Patterns of Culture*. Boston: Houghton Mifflin Company, 1934.

Cairncross, F. *The Death of Distance*. London: Orion Business Books, 1997.

DeLubac, Henri. *Further Paradoxes*. London: Longmans, Green & Co., 1958.

DeThomasis, Louis. *Social Justice: A Christian Pragmatic Response in Today's World*. Winona, MN: Saint Mary's University of Minnesota, 1982.

DeThomasis, Louis, and William Ammentorp. *Paradigms and Parables: The Ten Commandments for Ethics in Business*. Amherst, MA: Human Resource Development Press, 1995.

Friedman, Milton. *Capitalism and Freedom*. Chicago: University of Chicago Press, 1962.

Friedman, Thomas. *The World is Flat*. New York: Farrar, Straus & Giroux, 2005.

Geertz, Clifford. *After the Fact*. Cambridge, MA: Harvard University Press, 1996.

Hall, Edward T. *Beyond Culture.* New York: Anchor Books, 1976.

Jenkins, Joe. *Ethics and Religion.* Oxford: Heinemann, 1999.

Jenkins, Philip. *The Next Christendom: The Coming of Global Christianity.* New York: Oxford University Press, 2002.

Jones, Donald G., ed. *Doing Ethics in Business.* Cambridge, MA: Oelgeschlager, Gunn & Hain, 1982.

LaFollette, Hugh. *Ethics in Practice: An Anthology.* Oxford: Blackwell, 1997.

Lewis, Bernard. *Holy Wars and Unholy Terror.* New York: The Modern Library, 2003.

Maxwell, John C. *There's No Such Thing as "Business" Ethics.* New York: Warner Books, 2003.

McEwan, Tom. *Managing Values and Beliefs in Organizations.* Essex, England: Pearson Education Limited, 2001.

Merlean-Ponty, Maurice. *Humanism and Terror.* Boston: Beacon Press, 1969.

McNeill, Daniel, and Paul Freiberger. *Fuzzy Logic: The Revolutionary Computer Technology That Is Changing Our World.* New York: Simon & Schuster, 1993.

Minogue, Kenneth. *Alien Powers: The Pure Theory of Ideology.* New York: St. Martin's Press, 1985.

Morrison, Toni. *Beloved.* New York: Penguin Books, 1987.

Nuttall, Jon. *Moral Questions: An Introduction to Ethics.* Oxford: Blackwell, 1997.

Shepherd, Linda. *Lifting the Veil: The Feminine Face of Silence.* Boston: Shambhala, 1993.

Trusted, Jennifer. *Moral Principles and Social Values.* London: Routledge Kegan Paul, Ltd., 1987.

Whyte, William Foote, and Kathleen King Whyte. *Making Mondragon: The Growth and Dynamics of the Worker Cooperative Complex.* Ithaca, NY: ICR Press, Cornell University, 1988.

Young, Stephen. *Moral Capitalism.* San Francisco: Berrett-Kohler Publishers, Inc., 2003.

Index